Power of Transparency

A Guide to Balance
Business Ownership and Motherhood

Lisa Liberatore

Transparency Enterprises

Printed in the United States of America
First edition, Softcover
Print: ISBN 978-0-9989881-0-8
ISBN 978-0-9989881-1-5
E-book: 978-0-9989881-2-2

Library of Congress Control Number: 2017907516

Edited by Carrol Lange
Book design by E. Mae Media Arts

Acknowledgements

This book is dedicated to Dorian Maxwell and his dad. Without them, this book couldn't have been written.

My family for their unconditional love and support.

Kelly McClymer for her guidance and encouragement.

Contents

Transparency in Hiring   1

Juggling a Baby with Burritos   9

Create Your Culture   19

When Your Business & Personal
            Life Become Blurred   23

Get Creative with Your Financing   27

Believe in the Power to Dream Even Bigger   31

The End of a Marriage   39

The Culture I Created Helped Me
            Through Difficult Times   43

Navigating the End   47

Managing Expectations   53

Diversify Your Network   59

Know Your Management Style   69

Change Your Hire/Fire Mindset   75

Transparency Networking   83

Unintentional Networking Can
            Generate Big Rewards   95
The Importance of Feedback   103
Fiscal Responsibility   107
Self Care   113
Details Matter   123
Free to Find Me   127
Blending Work and Family   137
Support   141
Celebrating the Next Chapter   147
What Transparency Looks Like in Real Life   151
Epilogue   159

Foreword

Are you ready to achieve a better integration of your personal and work life? Are you looking for ways to do it all, without feeling so drained? If you picked up this book, I know you are! If you're a mom and a business owner or a career woman, *Power of Transparency* can guide your way, bringing together all the different facets of your life to form a whole that is bigger than the sum of its parts.

I met Lisa when she opened CoVort, a co-working space in Bangor, Maine. After joining, Lisa and I found out we had a lot in common. Here was another divorced mom with not only one business, but many. We connected instantly! Lisa is a female serial entrepreneur, or mompreneur, a term the media likes to use. After getting to know Lisa, *wow*, did my perspective on what I could accomplish change!

Lisa's first business was Baxter Tea, a company she opened in 2007 and successfully sold in 2012. She opened and still retains an ownership stake in Lisa's Legit Burritos, which has two locations through a licensing agreement. She is also the co-founder of CoVort, a co-working space for remote workers and business start-ups, and is a Managing Partner of Fractional Executives of ME, a technical consulting company.

When she decided to write a book, she didn't just write a book. She took the leap and decided to self-publish. She created a website, blog, podcast, YouTube channel and a publishing company as well. She trademarked her logo. She laid the groundwork to profit from the fruits of her labors rather than letting others gain from her efforts. Most importantly, she didn't dwell on making the book perfect. She just did it. What an inspiration!

What makes me qualified to give Lisa and her book such rave reviews? I'm 38. I'm a mom of 3. My ex-husband and I co-parent using a nesting style. I am an employer and own several businesses including Crooked Steeple Hall. I am the happiest and most successful I've ever been, and my friendship with Lisa is a major contributing factor.

In the past, I was a victim of imposter syndrome. I never felt good enough. I still feel that way sometimes, but through Lisa, I've learned a few things: to stop worrying about the what-if's and JUST DO IT, to ask for and rely on help from others, to trust that people are good and want to see you succeed, to keep positive people around you and let the negative ones go, and most importantly, to be transparent in both your business and personal life.

It's been a whirlwind year to say the least! I wouldn't be where I am now without Lisa. I was stuck in a holding pattern and her blunt style encouraged me to move forward. Her friendship and mentorship have taken me leaps and bounds ahead of where I ever thought I would be at this point in my life.

Lisa's book, *Power of Transparency*, can help you turn the tide in your life as well. If you are feeling overwhelmed trying to balance work and life, if you have a business idea and aren't sure where start, or if you already own a business and want to take it to the next level this book is for you. If you have a career you love, but find your personal life overwhelming, this book is for you too! Lisa's personal stories, along with her specific tips and take-aways, provide an excellent strategy to help you get you going.

I'm so excited you're reading this book and I know you will get as much out of it as I did. Lisa shares her common struggles and demonstrate how to work through them. Take Lisa's advice - you will be glad you did. Here's to rocking your business and being an awesome mom at the same time!

Katrina Petersen

Introduction

Before we can start this conversation, I need to define what the word *transparency* means to me.

I use transparency to mean the ability to be open about what is going on in the moment. There are different levels of openness, but at its core, it's using honesty with those around you to build trust.

Transparency allows others to know that your distraction is not a result of something to do with them and does not need to be taken personally. Transparency short circuits miscommunication. Using it will help you identify how you feel in the moment without assigning blame.

Traditional business wisdom suggests hiding your emotions while doing business. The problem with that approach is unless you are super skilled at hiding your feelings (and you're not!), people sense that something is going on and start to wonder if they upset you. That speculation can change the communication dynamic for the worse.

My approach: if you're having a bad day, don't sugar coat it. When someone asks me how I am, I share one of several possible answers based on the level of friendship. For example, I can tell anyone that my car blew a tire on the way to a meeting. When talking about more personal issues, such as visiting a dying friend or problems with tenants, I am vague but clear. This allows me to share information with everyone, even with those I don't know well.

Transparency starts with honesty, admitting that you don't have all the answers, and a commitment to seek out solutions. By living a transparent life, you not only communicate what your needs are, but you explain your reasoning and its impact on whatever is at hand. When you need help, people will be able to give you step-by-step advice. Because they know what you've done so far, they'll be able to pinpoint where you went wrong or provide targeted guidance.

You dramatically reduce the amount of mental chatter that goes on when you live a transparent life. What you see is what you get. If someone is unsure of anything, your transparency provides the safety to ask questions or clarify.

Most importantly, transparency offers others an understanding of your thought process methodology, as well as what informs your decision making. As a result, you are more likely to receive buy-in, the foundation of solid relationships.

Practicing transparency is not always easy, but the reward of doing so is great.

Timeline

2007 - Baxter Tea Company was founded

2010 - Baxter Tea Company opens a
retail location

2011 - Lisa's Legit Burritos was founded

2012 - Baxter Tea Company is sold

2012 - Dorian is born

2013 - 2nd Lisa's Legit Burritos location opens

2014 - Ian leaves

2015 - Created a licensing agreement for Lisa's
Legit Burritos

Transparency in Hiring

"Good business leaders create a vision, articulate the vision, passionately own the vision, and relentlessly drive it to completion."

- Jack Welch,
Former CEO of GE

When I was 34 weeks pregnant, my restaurant manager gave notice. A mother herself, Ann knew firsthand the demands of raising young children and running her own small business. She'd spent the previous eight months trying to help me understand the complexities of being a business owner and a new mom. She knew it was not as pure and idealistic as I imagined, and she did her best to help prepare me for a new reality.

I'd initially hired Ann based on a friend's recommendation, and boy, was I lucky to find her! Her cheerful personality and easy ability to connect with people made everyone feel welcome. She was a fantastic representation of the brand I was working to build, and I knew replacing her wouldn't be easy. She had been with Lisa's Legit Burritos (LLB) since it's earliest days and had made invaluable contributions to the business. She helped shape systems still in place, and her sense of ownership and belonging was strong. I'd learned a lot from watching her engage with people. She was a true community builder.

Ann cried when she shared she had accepted a position with full benefits and vacation time. She loved LLB, and with only two weeks to replace her, she knew I was screwed!

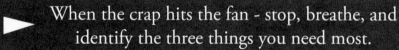

When the crap hits the fan - stop, breathe, and identify the three things you need most.

The news of Ann leaving combined with the smell of chicken cooking made me run to the bathroom. I felt annoyed, resentful, and guilty for feeling that way. Mine was not a planned pregnancy, nor was I excited to be pregnant. I'd worked hard to achieve my educational and professional goals, and I'd spent some time in the child development field. I was aware many couples try for a long time to have a baby, but for me, the timing felt completely wrong.

While I knew that the standard process for filling a managerial position usually takes about six weeks from the job posting to completion of training, I didn't have that much time. My baby was almost due. I had to fast track the process by focusing on my top three criteria for the position. I needed someone *reliable, independent* and whose *personality and style fit my brand*. Mine wasn't just another quick serve restaurant. LLB was a place where we greeted customers by name and started orders when we saw our regulars parking their cars.

Cast a wide net. ◀

In the past, when something like this happened, I would just jump in and carry every shift - open until close - until I figured things out. But I was about to have a baby, and that was not going to work. I felt scared and desperate. I posted on Facebook that LLB was hiring. With adrenaline rushing and hormones raging, I added "MUST be available NIGHTS AND WEEKENDS. If you aren't, please don't bother applying. I am 34 weeks pregnant and need to hire someone ASAP."

As soon as I hit 'Post,' I realized I'd probably broken all kinds of human resources rules with my language, but the world needed to know I was serious about bringing on someone who was dedicated and who could appreciate the daunting task ahead of me. I was preparing to juggle a newborn and business still in its toddler years. During this time, I was most afraid that my baby boy would arrive before I could train a new manager.

I was confident I could find someone to be a "warm body." But could I find someone with the ability to operate truly independently while I was laying in a hospital bed? This concern was a major stressor.

Adding to my worry, my cash flow position did not afford me the possibility of having two people on the books to facilitate training if it wasn't completed before I went on leave. I had to act quickly and decisively to give myself the best shot at finding the right person in a short amount of time.

 Be prepared

The applications were printed and ready to be filled out. I knew I could train every aspect of the business. The one thing I couldn't teach was a manager's ability to make people feel welcome and excited to eat at LLB. When anyone came into the restaurant to apply, I immediately evaluated the connection between that person and the brand I had worked tirelessly to create.

Trust your gut. ◀

Jen, 31, was so nervous she was shaking. I could tell she was trying to relax, but her discomfort was obvious. I gave her an application and kept her talking. She described her great culinary background. To add to that, she was a mom herself and a diehard LLB fan who LOVED our pork tacos. Based on her level of nervousness, I asked her to say more about her work history. She hadn't interviewed or worked outside the home for some years, a time she spent raising her son.

She left, and I struggled with her application. She seemed to possess the necessary culinary skills, but I wondered how she'd be with customers. Her ability to connect with me - although it took a little longer than I would have liked - was critical in my decision to take a chance on her. During our interview, I had observed her warm, friendly personality and discovered she had a great sense of humor, so I decided to go with my gut. I hired her and prayed my intuition was spot on. This was not the time for it to fail me. I didn't bother with reference checks. Instead, I focused on trusting my instincts. I scheduled a time for her to come in, complete the necessary new hire paperwork and begin training. On day one, I gave her the keys to my kingdom and let her know how much I was relying on her to carry LLB while I did the whole "new mom" thing.

Jen's warmth and personality blossomed during her brief training, and within a few years, she grew to become the backbone of the restaurant, affectionately calling it "the salsa mine" and jokingly referring to her coworkers as "her children." The restaurant continues to be successful, full of her joy and creative energy!

"LLB is a truly unique and magical place. I'm not just talking about that feeling of biting into a pork taco and feeling all of the flavors dance the Charleston on your tongue. This place changes lives. It certainly changed mine. I applied on a whim. It was close to home, I have a passion for burritos and Mexican food in general, and at the time I was just looking for something a few hours a week to supplement my husband's income. A little over three years later, LLB is basically my love. If LLB is Lisa's baby, I've been the wet nurse feeding, loving, and trying to nurture it in her absence. Our staff is small but comprised of a gaggle of amazing people."

-Jen

Juggling a Baby with Burritos

"Take the time to come home to yourself every day."

-Robin Casarjean

Dorian Maxwell was born on a Taco Tuesday at 4 am. I was 39 weeks pregnant. The day before, at what would be my last prenatal appointment, my doctor asked me if I had any questions. As usual, I replied "no."

Then she looked me straight in the eye and said, "You know, you're having this baby soon, and your life will completely change. You haven't asked a single question in 8 months! Are you sure you don't have *any* questions?"

"It's ok," I said. "I'm going to wear my baby while I work; I'll figure it all out as it comes. I've got this! My attention needs to be focused on my restaurant and making sure it's going to be ok without me for a few days."

"You can't bring a newborn to work!" she incredulously replied.

I finally had a question! "Well, how soon *can* I bring him to work?

"Three weeks," she said.

But being a small business owner, I knew there was no way I could stay away from my business that long.

On day 3, we went home from the hospital. I nursed Dorian, left my husband Ian in charge, and drove down to LLB to check on things. I knew everything was okay. I'd been in communication with my staff while I was laying in a hospital bed. I was a sore, exhausted, hormonal mess whose boobs had bled while breastfeeding, but I missed being at work! I'd been a mom for three days now. I wanted to return to my comfort zone and desperately needed to experience "normal." For me, that was being at LLB.

Every day, before or after hours, I'd leave Dorian with Ian for a short time and go in to take care of the bookkeeping. I made runs to the local grocery store to pick up miscellaneous items, did the ordering, and processed payroll. I wasn't there for very long, maybe 30-60 minutes. It felt so good to be in control of something again.

My employees and the other downtown merchants told me I was crazy for being at work and that I needed to get back to my son. They followed their comments with the question, "Why didn't you bring your brown-eyed baby with you?"

> My internal struggle between wanting to be a full-time mom *and* a business owner was an ongoing battle.

As soon as three weeks came around, Dorian and I were in the restaurant together. It was only a few hours at a time, and I was mostly taking orders and chatting with customers. It fed my soul to be back and part of the LLB team. But every time I worked, I felt a rise of anxiety and an impending sense of dread. I prayed it wouldn't be crazy busy while I was there. "How I was going to handle it?" I worried Dorian would cry, or worse yet, have one of his diaper blowouts that required an immediate bath and outfit change. Then suddenly, my business brain would kick in, reminding me that LLB needed to be busy to stay open. I'd figure things out.

One of the bonuses of being transparent with people was that many of my customers felt like friends. When the restaurant was swamped, and I needed to jump in and help fill orders, I would ask someone waiting if they wanted to hold Dorian. It was incredible how quickly people said yes. I would run behind the counter, make their food, and then exchange a burrito for a baby.

I also made friends with the ladies at the GirlTrend Shop, a consignment boutique next door to LLB. Sarah, one of the owners, even kept toys on hand for Dorian. If he got too cranky next door, Sarah would bring him back and say, "Sorry, I tried." I'd thank her, take a deep breath, and choke back the tears. In those moments, I felt like I had failed both my staff and my baby. I'd apologize to the whole restaurant as I took a seat in the dining room to assess if Dorian just needed mommy cuddles or if we needed to head home for a few hours.

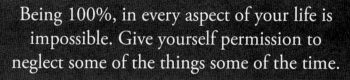

> Being 100%, in every aspect of your life is impossible. Give yourself permission to neglect some of the things some of the time.

I wanted so badly to do everything at once without anything being out of balance. That wasn't reality. I had a baby. I now understood that he would always trump everything else. What I was doing was the very definition of juggling! With a baby in tow, moms never know what the day - or hour - will bring. You have to hold on and adjust on the fly. I magnified my stress because I chose to spend our days at the restaurant, where we lacked a back office escape. As soon as we got to the restaurant, we were "on." My staff was beyond accommodating. There were times they would tell me to go home, reassuring me that they could handle everything.

> As soon as I accepted the fact that the life I had pre-Dorian wasn't going to return, I needed to make some significant changes, including asking for help.

I missed my independence and would often ask one of the staff if they would take Dorian so I could take orders and make food. Yes, I asked my employees to NOT do the job I'd hired them to do because I wanted so desperately to be FREE, but I didn't want my son too far from me. I chose a difficult path. My vision of being a full-time mom and a full-time business owner involved a lot of help from other people. I guess you could say I had a whole network of "nannies" that helped me raise him.

My friend Eliza had a similar experience. Her vision of being a candy store owner with a baby in tow was almost immediately thrown out. She told me it was deeply upsetting to learn her dream of seamlessly combining work and motherhood wasn't a reality. She didn't anticipate needing to ask for help, but when things didn't turn out the way she hoped, she was lucky she had family who were there to support her. She found ways to adapt and accepted she had to utilize whatever resources were available to her to keep things running smoothly.

> Flexibility is essential.
> When help is offered, take it.

Follow Your Curiosity
The GirlTrend Shop

"You can have everything you want in life if you just help enough people get what they want in life."

-Zig Ziglar

Sarah and Megan were best friends who loved to shop at a local consignment boutique next door to the restaurant. The business went up for sale, and they purchased it on a whim. They had no experience. They loved it and thought "why not?" They shared a great eye for fashion and knew what would sell. The prior owner handed them a piece of paper with some sales numbers and paperwork on consignors. No manual laid out how to operate the business. Sarah admits she didn't ask many questions before the purchase. She didn't even know what to ask. They had a vision for the way they wanted the store to look, but the backend - the operational piece - was underdeveloped, to put it mildly.

I stopped by to welcome them to the downtown and asked a few questions out of curiosity. I love learning about different businesses and was interested to gain more knowledge about owning a consignment shop. I asked a few basic questions and received either no answer or an answer lacking an understanding of the reason behind it.

For example, I asked, "Why are you processing your consignors in that way?" Their answer was "Because that's how the sellers gave it to us in the sale." With no analysis of the "why" behind anything, my questions caused Sarah and Megan to look more deeply into what it means to run a business. They had the passion and the drive, and like many entrepreneurs, they jumped out of the plane and planned to build their parachutes on the way down. They invited me into their business to offer guidance and share resources. When I asked about their insurance coverage, they told me they didn't have a policy and asked, "Who do you use?" I got on the phone right then and there and made an introduction. The need for insurance coverage was critical!

"Lisa was super helpful even though she had her own business, a baby, and a chaotic home life. She was more than willing to say, 'I can help with that.' She truly wanted us to succeed. She knew if we grew, she would grow. Her focus was always on the community and how she could help improve the bottom line of those around her so everyone would prosper. She helped us grow personally and got our business on track. She truly cared, and a lasting friendship developed through her curiosity about the new owners next door."

- Sarah, Co-owner,
The GirlTrend Shop

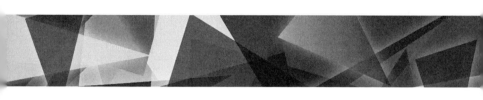

Create Your Culture

"People want to be recognized. They want to be celebrated in some way. They want to be made to feel as if they do count for something. And they want a place where they can belong in the community that stands for something more than just an enterprise that makes money."

-Martin Coles,
Starbucks International President

I grew up in an Italian home where we greeted guests with hugs. As I got to know my restaurant customers, a lot of hugging started to happen!

I wanted a warm and welcoming atmosphere. I invited my customers to hang their artwork on the walls, and my window displays changed with the seasons. I genuinely enjoyed serving delicious food to hungry people. Owning a restaurant was a perfect fit for me, and it showed. I valued every customer who came through the door, and I made certain my staff did also. This attitude and commitment set us apart.

Customers told me they liked coming in because they felt like they were a part of the LLB family. Many became personal friends, including one that went on to babysit Dorian. We knew where our customers worked and what their hobbies were and how they were doing - because we asked! On their days off, some would show up with their families in tow. It was amazing.

We made it a habit of memorizing the orders of our regulars. As soon as they came in, we'd ring them up and get to work. We regularly asked for customer feedback and took suggestions for our menu. These little details make a huge impact in building customer loyalty.

LLB participated in downtown events and played an active role in community engagement. One such event, the Gardiner ArtWalk, brought hundreds of people to our space in an evening. Those nights were the most fun. Our little restaurant was at max capacity all night, but everyone was in such a great mood. No matter how hard my staff was working, they were smiling. It was an awesome feeling.

> ## Shift the culture when a baby arrives. ◀

After Dorian was born, Lisa's Legit Burritos saw some significant changes. I viewed the restaurant as an extension of myself, and I wanted my business to reflect who I was. If I was going to spend the majority of my time there, I needed to feel comfortable.

> ## You can't always control your environment, but you can control how you respond to it. ◀

I brought in a bouncy seat and high chair and collected some toys in a cardboard lettuce box. I made the environment child-friendly to meet my needs and saw a positive shift in our business culture. LLB had always been a laid back restaurant, but with these changes, it became a particularly attractive option for parents with young kids.

It's your business - make changes when you need to.

The feedback was terrific. Parents said:

"We missed going out to eat and are so thankful you're here."

"Your food is healthy and ready fast, and it's ok if the kids play with the toys while we finish eating."

"We don't get dirty looks from the staff if our kids make a mess."

It's just a mess - you can clean it up!

Dorian was the king of throwing stuff off of his high-chair and smearing black beans everywhere. He helped my staff understand what life with babies and young kids looks like: messy. Enjoying a meal out as a parent isn't an easy feat. Everyone is trying their hardest. I once over-heard a customer apologizing for the mess made by her child. As she attempted to clean up, my employee joked with her and explained the mess was minor compared to the ones made by the owner's son. It was great to see the stress disappear from her face!

When Your Business & Personal Life Become Blurred

"Courage starts with showing up and letting ourselves be seen."

- Brené Brown.

We dubbed Dorian LLB's "CEO, " and we featured him prominently in our marketing materials. I had officially brought the public into my private life, and there was no turning back!

I'd always been very open and honest with people. Most of my customers knew where my husband worked and would hear a bit about our adventures. But when we added a child, who became the face of our business, we invited a deeper level of connection with our customers.

Everyone seemed to be able to connect with Dorian. He enjoyed being on the go and seeing lots of people. Our customers took such an interest. If folks knew Dorian had a cold, the next time they were in they asked how he was feeling. Patrons and I discussed everything from sleep training to vaccinations. No matter the age of my customer's kids, I heard stories of when they were Dorian's age. I loved connecting through the common bond we now shared, and I received a lot of valuable advice.

Sarah, a stay at home mom, came in every few weeks with her adorable, blonde haired, blued eyed daughter, Natalie. They'd have lunch, check out our used book section and chat with me about local happenings. It was very exciting when I learned she and I were pregnant at the same time - both with boys!

Time passed and as cute as he was, having Dorian at

the restaurant eventually became a distraction and liability. No longer would he cuddle in a customer's arms while I made their food. Instead, he was a tornado and into everything. Facing budgetary constraints and still desiring to spend as much time with him as possible, I reached out to my customer turned friend, Sarah.

Ask for help! ◀

People want to help, but not enough people JUST ASK. Maybe it's how society has trained us, or maybe we don't feel we have anything to give in return, but I've learned a different way. When someone asks me for help, I'm immediately flattered to be considered a resource. I spring into action with a big smile on my face and say, "YES! How can I help?"

For example, a fellow downtown business owner came in for lunch one day and asked for advice. He was unsure of the best way to handle the volume of donation requests his shop received. He wanted to be a good community member, but he didn't want to go broke in the process. I told him he wasn't alone in feeling conflicted.

I'd developed a plan at LLB to address this issue, and I was happy to share it. We required organizations seeking donations to complete a request form and provide a nonprofit EIN (Employee Identification Number) for tax purposes. We asked for 30 days notice, and we made sure solicitors understood that we had a donation budget. They knew once it was spent, we couldn't do more. This strategy worked well for us and other small businesses as well.

Get Creative with Your Financing

"Whatever your income, always live below your means."

-Thomas J. Stanley,
The Millionaire Next Door

My husband and I opened our first restaurant using our modest personal savings. We didn't take out any loans. Because funds were limited and the risk was high, I knew I had to be thorough when creating the startup budget and drafting cash flow projections. There was no room for error. I needed to know down to the number of serving spoons what this venture was going to cost.

My research began with visiting Mexican restaurants throughout the state. I tasted the food, analyzed menus, and studied kitchen and dining room layouts. From there, I crafted my menu and made a list of necessary equipment. As luck would have it, the building we found to house Lisa's Legit Burritos had 85% of what we needed, and they sold it to us for pennies on the dollar.

▶ Just ask.

When it came time to open LLB's 2nd location, we had to purchase everything outright. I stalked Craigslist and every other website I could find searching for deals. Ian, Dorian and I once drove 2.5 hours to Old Orchard Beach to load up a bunch of tables when I spotted a discarded hand washing sink on the ground nearby. I asked the seller what his plan was for the sink. "Oh, you can have it. I bought a new one and was going to throw the old one out." I decided to ask what else he was going to throw out, and sure enough, we walked away with a lot of additional equipment - and helpful advice - for free. Having raised his family while running a restaurant, he appreciated our ambitious undertaking and was eager to see us succeed.

> It doesn't have to be
> shiny - it just needs to work.

It's better to get a year out of a piece of equipment and be debt free than go into debt for years. Instead, deposit what you'd have paid every month if you'd financed the purchase. This fund will help cover the cost of future repair or replacement.

Believe in the Power to Dream Even Bigger

"Whatever the mind can conceive and believe, the mind can achieve."

— Dr. Napoleon Hill,
Think and Grow Rich

After the first few months of learning to run a business and take care of an infant, my confidence grew dangerously high. Dorian was perfectly happy to sit in his car seat and watch the world go by at the restaurant. He was sleeping through the night, which meant I was, too.

I happened to see my friend Tobias at a networking event and proudly told him how well LLB was doing. He mentioned that the tenants in his downtown Augusta property had given their notice. He was aware of my knack for 'spreading the word' and hoped I might help him find new tenants to join the revitalization effort that was starting to occur in his community. I said to him, half-jokingly, "Maybe I'll open a second location."

His eyes lit up at the thought of an LLB in downtown Augusta. He cajoled me with tempting facts for a restaurant owner: there were very few options for people to grab a quick lunch downtown, a new courthouse was being built just steps away, and a call center next door employed over 100 people.

> **Dream in the presence of those who will help you achieve.**

Tobias' passion was contagious. He got me thinking BIG again. But was I ready for a second restaurant? I told him I'd have to talk things over with Ian. I secretly thought

I should have known better than to express my inner dialogue in front of him! Ever since first meeting him, Tobias had inspired a sense of competitiveness in me. He saw me as someone capable of accomplishing great things. His enthusiasm and belief in me fed my drive to prove him right.

I'd already successfully run my coffee and tea company and then again expanded my skillset opening LLB. I was confident in the systems I built in Gardiner and thought it would be an easy transition from one restaurant location to two. Running into Tobias at this juncture felt serendipitous.

I was still suffering from the naïveté of being a new mom, however. If Dorian had been mobile at the time, my decision might have been different. His quiet nature as an infant allowed me to have a sense of confidence that I guarantee I wouldn't have had if I had run into Tobias even six months later.

Know when to call in backup. ◀

Ian was willing to entertain the idea of a second restaurant as well, so I scheduled a time to meet up with Tobias and his contractor to take a tour of the space. We weren't committing ourselves to anything, only exploring the possibilities. We had to rely pretty heavily on our imaginations because the place was gross. It housed old, stained carpet, drop ceilings, the world's smallest, non-ADA bathroom and electric heat that was costing hundreds of dollars a month to operate.

My practical nature recognized the place was in need of a complete overhaul, but its view of the Kennebec River was beautiful. Tobias, sensing my dismay and knowing how much work I'd have to put into place, got up on a ladder and pulled a few of the ceiling tiles aside to reveal a tin ceiling in mint condition.

Wondering what I was getting myself into, I tried to be realistic with him. Ian and I couldn't afford to do all the renovations required to convert the space into a restaurant, let alone restore the historical aspects of the building. But Tobias believed in me and was willing to work out a deal. He invested in some capital improvements, including installing a new heating/cooling system and windows. Ian and I agreed to do the rest of the work and didn't pay rent during the renovations. I was open and honest about my financial limitations, and as a result, we found a way to work together to make it a win/win.

I could see the new LLB in my mind's eye as I wrestled with the details of opening a second location. Fortunately, having both vision and some experience on my side helped me negotiate a relatively low-risk deal. We signed a five-year lease with no security deposit required. Instead, we used those funds for improvement projects and helped increase the value of his property.

Ian and I talked about the logistics of two locations and decided that we would each run a restaurant. He had been teaching Industrial Arts at a local high school but believed our work/life balance would benefit if we could both have a flexible schedule and keep our son with us most of the time.

When we began renovations, our goal was for Ian to run the Augusta location while I focused on Gardiner. I'd still oversee LLB's big picture, but he would be the owner representation in Augusta. One thing I had learned while running LLB Gardiner was how important it is for owners to have a presence in their Main Street businesses.

Do your best - there is always tomorrow.

The juggling act of running a location with a baby in tow plus overseeing the construction of a second restaurant (including the all important decor buying spree), was a real test of my ability to multitask. There were days when I would lay down at night and couldn't believe how much I'd done. I felt like a super mompreneur!

The pendulum would swing, of course. There were days when Dorian just needed to be home. I'd cry when I looked at the long list of things that didn't get accomplished. Dorian was my priority, so I'd ask my staff to run errands for me instead of dragging him out, or I'd ask the contractor to pick up materials I'd promised to deliver to the job site.

Assess your situation frequently and remain flexible.

When I started to feel stress creeping in, I didn't fight the feeling and try to push it away. Instead, I would stop and take a moment to try to understand the source of it (if any). Ultimately, I decided to harness my feelings and let them motivate me to do what I needed to do. A positive action would always allow some stress to resolve and release.

For example, I'd wake up in the middle of the night anxious about all the things that needed to be done. My mind was racing, wondering if the cash flow projection I created was right, or whether or not I'd find the perfect piece of art to tie the place together. I worried about spending enough "quality" time with Dorian. He was attached to my hip, but was I playing with him enough?

"If we are positive and concerned (not to be confused with worried), our brains are able to expand, allowing for faster processing and increased productivity."
– Shawn Achor

Believe in the Power to Dream Even Bigger

I used my 'midnight mini freak out sessions' to channel my energy into making lists. While I recognized I wasn't going to resolve issues in the moment and that sleep was necessary, I knew I'd feel better if I made a list and fired off a couple of emails. I kept a separate list of people I needed to connect with who could help me achieve my goals. On another page, I'd write down my feelings, always recognizing my good fortune. I felt grateful to be feeling stressed by my new venture. I acknowledged my courage and determination and gave myself credit for doing something most people do not accomplish in a lifetime. I also reminded myself that nothing worth having comes without obstacles.

It is through the challenging times that I have learned and become a better professional. I understand the lessons of any given situation can - and likely will - be reference points in the future. I've observed that if I'm consistent with my journaling, I sleep better. If I do wake up, it's often to write down the solution to a problem I'd been struggling to solve.

In the end, with lots of bargain shopping for restaurant equipment and many hours of sweat equity, we opened a second location just days before Dorian's 1st birthday. Tobias was one of our first customers. By working together, he and I helped each other achieve individual goals. He found a great tenant for his building and LLB was getting a chance to expand!

The End of a Marriage

"Always remember you are braver than you believe, stronger than you seem, and smarter than you think."

- A. A. Milne,
Winnie the Pooh

On a sunny day in September, the day after Dorian's 2nd birthday, I watched my husband pull out of our driveway, our car packed with his belongings. As I closed and locked the door, I felt a sense of calm rush over me. The turbulence of the past year was finally over.

I didn't have a fucking clue what I was going to do, and my mind was racing in a million directions, but I did know Ian wouldn't be waking me at 2 am after playing a gig at a bar. I no longer needed to worry if he was ok when he didn't come home on time, or feel resentful while he slept in when I'd been up several times through the night with our son.

> ▶ You knew things weren't good - but seriously - did that just happen?!

My first call was to my little sister, Maria. She was getting her Ph.D. in physical therapy and had lived with us for two summers while doing rotations in central Maine. She'd seen firsthand the inner workings of my marriage. I knew I didn't have to say much for her to understand the situation. She said, "Ok, I'm jumping in the car. I'll be there in an hour." Before I knew it, she'd called my mom and other sister in Portland.

You couldn't beat my support system! My sister arrived with a pizza from my favorite place and a 12 pack of beer.

She told me to sit down and eat, and she'd feed Dorian and give him a bath. My parents immediately volunteered to pay for the best lawyer in Maine - they were ready for battle. I wasn't sure if Ian and I were heading toward divorce, or if we'd just entered another 'rough patch' in our marriage.

Right away, I had to make everyone, including myself, take a deep breath. I needed my family to understand I had to do this my way. It was unconventional, but I had a gut feeling that as much I hated the fact that he left me, and while I deeply resented all the shit we'd been through, I knew Ian and I needed to manage our evolving circumstances by ourselves, with as little legal intervention as possible.

That night, after rocking Dorian to sleep, I went to my room and broke down. I cried for our child. He was going to have a very different life than the one I'd had. I was so thankful to have grown up with two loving parents, both in the same household. My dream of providing that experience for Dorian was now shattered. I mourned that loss, but I also understood that an unhappy home was no place to raise my son.

In that moment, I found peace. I felt a huge weight had been lifted from my shoulders. Dorian and I would begin a new chapter in our lives, and I was determined to make it a positive one.

The Culture I Created Helped Me Through Difficult Times

"To be yourself in a world that is constantly trying to make you something else is the greatest accomplishment."

- Ralph Waldo Emerson

As my personal life fell apart behind the scenes, I continued working and told myself "everything is fine" and "just keep going." There came a point, however, when I couldn't pretend anymore.

Juggling motherhood and business ownership is an incredible feat on its own. When I added the chaos and uncertainty of divorce, life became painful in private and overwhelming in public. I was all over the map emotionally.

▶ **It's worth it to be open with people.**

There are many preconceptions about how a business person should operate. Some people believe you should keep a wall between your personal and business life. My instinct told me otherwise.

▶ **Transparency is a spectrum.**

When my marriage was ending, I initially held out on sharing information with my staff and customers because I was still coming to grips with it myself. However, my level of transparency changed throughout the process. Eventually, the emotional strain of keeping my impending divorce private wasn't worth it.

When I did finally share with people what was going on in my life, my already great relationships with staff and customers deepened. I felt I'd been set free, and I allowed myself to receive much-needed advice and support during a major life change.

 My ability to tell my customers what was happening helped me *and* exhausted me.

Inevitably, people began asking questions. I always did my best to choose my words carefully. I was surprised by the level of support and openness demonstrated by others. Many people shared their personal struggles, and that, in turn, helped me through my process. I appreciated their empathy, and I felt less alone.

Thankfully, my staff was quite protective of me. They offered me valuable feedback as I tried my best to find balance in my public-private life. At times, they were more aware of my need for privacy than I was. They let me know when someone asked too personal a question, or if they'd heard something gossipy 'on the street' about my divorce. They always had my back.

"While I was making his food, a customer said he'd heard Ian moved out. He wanted to know if it was true. I told him, "I don't know what's happening with Lisa at home, but here at work, she is a great boss and focused on the restaurant!"

- Manager, LLB

There isn't a formula for saying too much or saying too little. (But wouldn't ***that*** be nice to have?!)

At the end of the day, the decision to share sensitive information (and how much of it) is a deeply personal one. I recommend giving everyone around you a basic level of knowledge about what's happening. People are more likely to be understanding when they know when you're struggling.

Navigating the End

*"Forgiveness simply means loving
someone enough to pursue healing instead
of punishment when they have wronged you."*
— DaveWillis.org

When our relationship ended, Ian and I knew we needed to make sure we didn't kill ourselves financially with our divorce. We'd seen so many of our friends lose everything fighting each other in court. We were clear we didn't want to do things that way - it just wasn't smart.

It was an emotionally charged time, but we kept reminding ourselves to use the logical side of our brains and to do our best to keep emotions out of it. It was a challenge. We created communication and visitation ground rules for each other to help keep us on track, and we took our time researching the best way to untangle ourselves. I found a mediator in Portland who was willing to work with us for $160 per hour - much better than $300 per hour we'd each have paid separate lawyers.

Ian and I were committed to making sure Dorian didn't feel a seismic shift in the house. Most of Ian's visits with Dorian took place in our home, even when things between us were at their worst. There were many nights when, for Dorian's sake, we laid on a double mattress on the floor with Dorian between us, reading books and snuggling him until he was asleep. Then, Ian would walk out the door into the darkness, and I'd fall asleep, alone in our king sized bed, wondering what the hell had just happened.

A part of me was jealous that Ian got to go out and live his life while I was on duty when Dorian woke up in the middle of the night. I was pissed he got to sleep in while I dragged my tired body out of bed to serve our son breakfast and begin another physically and mentally exhausting day caring for a toddler. And yet, I could barely leave my son for a few hours to go to work. It was such a complex, no win feeling, one every mom I know feels. I learned even stay-at-home moms want time alone but feel guilty and disoriented without their children underfoot.

I felt very conflicted that Ian and I didn't have a clean break the way most people do when they separate and divorce, but everything we did was focused on what was best for Dorian and preserving our financial stability. We'd both worked so hard - we didn't want to hit the eject button and lose everything. We'd been very practical, and as business partners, we crushed it!

Ian and I knew it was wisest to work together to liquidate our assets and *make* money. We understood that emotionally based decisions were sure to lead to fire sales of our properties. I'll be honest, Ian was much better at not getting emotional (the way most guys are), but at the end of the day, my emotions were usually in check. I worked hard at consciously separating my thoughts and feelings, and I relied heavily on my family and friends for emotional support. Ending our marriage this way required a lot of faith and logic.

> Being emotionally aware is the first step to emotional management.

To engage your emotional intelligence, you must also be able to use your emotions to make effective decisions about your behavior. When you become overly stressed, you can lose control of your emotions and the ability to act thoughtfully and appropriately.

After Ian left, I chose to avoid the bar scene and relied instead on a having a couple of drinks with close friends to help relieve stress. I focused on sorting out the complex emotions that go along with divorce. Everyone deals with divorce differently. If you find that you need to 'let go' a little to alleviate stress, make sure you balance those activities in a healthy way.

I knew if I was going to move on, I needed to find peace with everything that had happened - I couldn't just sweep it under the rug and keep going full tilt with my life. Now was the time to do the hard work of piecing together the new me. For the first time in 12 years, I was alone.

I have always been a strong, independent person. I never took Ian's last name, but when we separated, I grieved the loss of our partnership. I realized just how much our distinct, separate lives had been blended by marriage.

There were times I'd just lie down and sob. I didn't fight the tears or the awful feeling of my heart aching. I knew my feelings were important to my healing process. I tried not to analyze why I was crying. The list was too long, and what I needed most in those moments was to release the pain.

▼

Following our separation, I realized very quickly I needed to step up my game as a business owner if I was going to maintain the lifestyle Ian and I had created. Once again, networking was critical during this transition. My ability to be honest with those in my inner circle meant I never had to ask for help. People close to me took it upon themselves to find ways to help ease my burden. I wasn't sure what steps to take next. I needed guidance, referrals, and help finding the ground under my feet.

I wasn't proud. I told people how it was. Life sucked! I was stressed and didn't know what the next day was going to bring. But I showed up and worked my ass off. I was determined to stay one step ahead of the earth as it crumbled behind me. A true entrepreneur, I was fueled by the mindset that I was just one misstep away from failure. I buckled down and worked harder than ever.

I was clear I was responsible for myself at this stage in my life. My parents had raised me on the promise of financial support until I was married or pregnant. I'd always taken it to heart, and it shaped how I saw everything. Now I was married and had a baby. I understood that my marriage - at it's best and at it's worst - was between Ian and me. Everyone else was on the outside. This situation was the ultimate test of my creativity. I would have to figure out the best way out of a circumstance I was partially responsible for creating. It takes two to have a marriage and two to dissolve one. I wasn't innocent, and I wanted to make sure I didn't play the role of victim.

Managing Expectations

"What screws us up most in life is the picture in our head of how it is supposed to be."

- Anonymous

After my divorce, I was a full-time single mom, an owner of 2 restaurants and on the board of several non-profits. While I tried my best to keep all these balls in the air, I knew it was only a matter of time before something (or everything) came crashing down.

It was obvious I needed to manage my expectations. This required me to accept that the life I had wasn't coming back. All of Ian's time, effort, and income, which had helped make us so successful, wasn't 'a thing' anymore. The realization was incredibly painful, but as soon as I accepted it, I was able to assess all facets of my life and strategically step back from some of my commitments.

> I wasn't yet at peace with my reality, but I knew denying it would just delay the hard work of starting my new life.

One night, after I'd put Dorian to sleep, I sat down on my king-sized bed. With a glass of red wine and a notebook, I took stock of my life. I recorded my assets, liabilities, board memberships, restaurant and real estate cash flow statements and the cost of running our home. All of these things were now my sole responsibility.

Before I knew it, the whole bed was covered with paperwork. Trying to make sense of it all caused a lot of anxiety, but I knew it had to be done to get clear about what changes were necessary. I'd seen so many people make emotionally charged decisions during the divorce process, and it never seemed to work out well. I was determined to keep my composure and to remain as logical as possible.

I'd sold my coffee and tea company during another time of intense change. Because of that experience, I was familiar with the process of closing chapters in my life and letting go of things I still loved and cherished in order to preserve my sanity. I recalled the freedom I'd ultimately felt following my initial sadness. It was worth it. I knew I had to go through it again and that some tough decisions needed to be made.

> Push back in a way that balances your needs and your commitments. ◀

Females are accustomed to putting everyone else's needs before their own. Divorce taught me I had to put myself first. I had to be sure that my family and business foundations were stable because, without me, life wouldn't be pretty.

It was tough to step away from the boards. I believed in their missions and felt I was letting them down. I'd started missing more and more meetings due to the up-heaval of my life, and I knew it wasn't fair to the other members or myself to continue in that fashion. Because I wasn't in a position to pull my weight, I felt I needed to make room for others who could help the organizations reach their goals.

It's been almost two years since I've served on a board. While I miss having that kind of involvement in my community, I know that overcommitting myself will only cause unnecessary stress.

Stay Focused on Your Initial Vision (Especially When Times Get Tough)

With Ian no longer running the Augusta location, I had to come up with a new routine that included a 20-minute drive between restaurants and a child with his napping schedule to consider. I juggled the upper management demands (ordering, accounting, and scheduling for each location) in addition to working or finding coverage when someone called out sick. Occasionally, I simply had to close the restaurant because I couldn't deal.

I'd pretty much given up on the notion of working behind the counter and was just trying to keep the doors open. I hated this transition! I missed having time to chat with my customers and catching up with my employees between rushes.

Although I believed in my restaurants, I felt like I was drowning trying to run them while also being a full-time, single mom. I kept them going while I explored ways to lessen the burden. Eventually, Dorian's needs and ten employees depending on my leadership was just too much. I broke down. I called my friend and mentor, Eliza. I told her I couldn't keep it up. Although I hated myself for even thinking it, I heard myself say, "I might close the restaurants."

Once you've made your vision a reality, it's easy to slip into autopilot mode. Then, when a crisis hits, it's common to panic and pull the plug.
DON'T!
Take a deep breath and remember your initial passion, the one that brought you this far.

Diversify Your Network

"The way to develop self-confidence is to do the thing you fear and get a record of successful experiences behind you."

- William Jennings Bryan

Eliza suggested I apply to Top Gun, a four-month business accelerator program offered by the Maine Center for Entrepreneurial Development. She'd participated in a previous session, and her business had benefited. She thought the program might help me create a road map to my new goal, a licensing agreement for the restaurants. This arrangement would allow me to maintain some ownership (and income!), but I wouldn't be responsible for day to day operations.

> The same passion and drive that helped me create LLB sustained me through the demands of the licensing agreement process.

Top Gun was a complex undertaking at an already stressful time. It required intense focus. The program introduced me to amazing mentors, advisors, and professionals who provided valuable guidance and quickly became key members of my network. Their support was crucial, but the real effort had to come from me. I used the tools of the program to rework my initial vision and shape it to fit my new reality. I gained a lot of confidence in the process.

> I'd already proven successful in establishing and running my restaurants. Now I was being fueled by an additional challenge: saving them.

During our first session, participants went around the room and talked about how we balanced our personal and professional lives. This was an ice-breaking exercise meant to set the tone for our conversations.

> Set an honest tone in your relationships.

Most people spoke about the challenges of starting a company, working long hours and not having a stable source of income. When it was my turn, I put it all out there. I told them I was a single mom who was trying to run two restaurants. I explained I was driving 1.5 hours to attend the program because I needed help creating an escape route while I dealt with a divorce and raising my son.

> People will mirror your level of openness.

The next person to speak said, "WOW! I can't complain about juggling life and business after hearing Lisa's story!"

My level of transparency sets me apart. When people are getting to know each other, especially in business, many maintain a facade. This just generates superficial relationships. I am willing to be open about my struggles in work and life. This makes others feel comfortable and safe to do the same.

> ## Your 'weakness' are opportunities to receive help.

Don't spend time trying to be great at something you aren't. Find people who have the knowledge and skills you lack and let them help you. Accept opportunities to learn more about yourself and your business. Always surround yourself with people who are smarter than you!

Top Gun was all about getting out from behind the counter and looking at the big picture of my business and how to grow it. It was a time of intense focus and connection making. Being in a formal program helped hold me accountable. I knew everyone else was working hard and achieving success and I wanted to also.

The Power of a Mentor Connection

Until this point, I was fortunate to have friends who turned into mentors such as Eliza and Tobias. I was connected to my first formal mentor during my time in Top Gun. The coordinator of the program made an introduction to Hugh via email. He's based in Texas, and his LinkedIn profile describes him as offering "a unique and diversified entrepreneurial perspective with a cumulative reputation for disciplined tenacity and professionalism; committed to leadership through excellence in service."

After exchanging a few pleasantries, Hugh cut to the chase and asked me to tell him about myself and my business. I started with my educational background then explained how I'd come up with the concept for LLB. I also shared how the restaurant had grown to two locations, had a baby, and was soon to be divorced.

> My personal life was the driving force behind my need for change.

I felt it was important to lay it all out there. I needed Hugh to see not only how the business worked, but why I was considering a licensing agreement. I didn't want to give up my trademark or lose complete control over something I'd worked so hard to create.

He explained what a franchise would entail and then gave me another option to explore - a licensing agreement. At the end of our first call, he assigned some homework. He asked me to think about what I really wanted and needed out of my business. He instructed me to play out some scenarios in my head and be prepared to discuss them next time we spoke.

It quickly became apparent to Hugh that I was serious and had the capability to pull off the process of creating and executing a licensing agreement. He was very impressed with the level of detail I'd developed for my restaurants thus far. In his experience, most business owners don't go through the painstaking process of documenting every aspect of their business or calculating the cost analysis down to a single napkin the way I had.

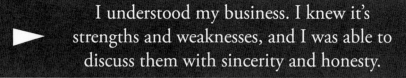

I understood my business. I knew it's strengths and weaknesses, and I was able to discuss them with sincerity and honesty.

Hugh was very clear that the licensing agreement process would be a tremendous amount of work and that it wouldn't be easy, but I was determined to do it.

After working with me to flesh out the rough concept, Hugh gave me the names of two lawyers. He told me to take the time to talk to both. Each was top notch, he explained, but I needed to make sure the one I chose was hearing me. This was the only way to ensure that the final document would reflect my desires.

Confused by his comments, I placed a call to the first lawyer. His receptionist scheduled a time the following week. When the time came to speak, it was clear that he was competent and had lots of experience executing what I wanted. However, he rushed through the meeting and only asked me a few questions. It was apparent that he wasn't interested in hearing my vision for how I wanted this to work. If I chose to work with him, it would be a very superficial relationship.

I called the second lawyer, and much to my surprise, he answered the phone. He was very pleasant and scheduled a time to take me out to lunch in Bangor. When I met him, he explained he was "swamped and not taking any new clients," but Hugh had recommended he talk with me.

We ended up working together. My lawyer took the time to understand me and the history of my business. The document he crafted accurately reflected my mission and vision. When the agreement was finished, the process of signing an engagement letter with an interested party was completed by the end of the next day.

Be open and honest. Guarded, superficial interactions do not build trust.

Hugh took me under his wing. Through his dedicated mentorship, he imparted valuable knowledge and helped me make some amazing connections. He changed the way I looked at my business and my capabilities. The "crazy" idea I thought was a pipe dream was actually a very REAL possibility. He kept pushing me to think bigger, beyond just two restaurants. He saw potential in me, and when I felt like throwing in the towel, he was there to pick me up and shove me toward success. He'd tell me to "quit bitching and get to work." Once I'd gained his confidence, there was NO taking my foot off the gas - it was full throttle 24/7. I had to make him proud.

After I'd signed the paperwork with my new business partners, Hugh said, "I never doubted your perseverance. I guess all the "I can't" you once communicated was just you screaming "watch me." Very impressive!"

> When trust is established, real change can happen quickly.

Top Gun teaches entrepreneurs to work on their businesses not just in them. Through the program, I realized that I wasn't the best person for managing the day to day operations of LLB. My strength as a professional was in building community and raising visibility. If my restaurants were going to prosper, I needed to step out of the way.

It was a slow transition. Incrementally, I gave more control and decision making power to my manager. Initially, it was very uncomfortable and scary, but the restaurant began to run more smoothly.

The process forced me to formally document all the steps required to complete everything from opening and closing the restaurant to what should be done during down time. If I wasn't going to be on site, I needed to make sure every detail was covered. I also had to find the right balance of communication with my staff, including establishing realistic expectations when I was away from the business. I was much like a nervous mom those first several times she leaves her baby in the care of another. In time, I began to accept that the restaurant was ok - I didn't need to keep asking.

"A mentor is someone who sees more talent and ability within you, than you see in yourself, and helps bring it out of you."

- Bob Proctor

Know Your Management Style

"Any executive, any CEO should not have one management style. Your management style needs to be dictated by your employees."
                                        - Keith Rabois

It's great to know your management style, but it does you no good if you're not aware of how your way of communicating and leading others affects your team.

For example, when a new hire came in for their first day of training, I'd ask them how they learn best. Would they prefer to watch me prepare food or would they be more comfortable reading our comprehensive training binder, which included step-by-step instructions for making our food? It's important to acknowledge that everyone learns differently. Identify what works best for each person and then make adjustments to ensure training is as pleasant and efficient as possible.

> Meet team members where they are and communicate in a style that resonates with them.

One of my employees was working alone, when I stopped in. She was just be standing around, feeling she'd done everything that needed to be done. Now, when you own a restaurant, there is always something that needs to be cleaned. As the saying goes, "If you have time to lean, you have time to clean." To address the issue, I came up with a list of tasks I wanted her to complete if she had time to spare during her shift. This worked very well for her, but other employees felt micromanaged and it adversely impacted their work.

> **A good leader adapts her style to the people with whom she is working.**

Create an environment where your employees feel comfortable, and they will be honest with you. This includes staying open to 'negative' feedback. They'll be more likely to give their all if they feel heard.

I created a culture where my employees knew they could talk to me about professional (or personal) challenges. I was empathetic. I offered advice and sometimes would help with accommodation at work.

> **Self-assessment is key.**

When you're the owner, you're always assessing your business and employees to make sure you are maximizing the operation. It's important to perform that same sort of "SWOT" (strengths, weaknesses, opportunities, threats) analysis on yourself.

"As soon as I began working at Lisa's Legit Burritos, my very first job, Lisa wanted to learn about my plans for after high school. When I told her I was not exactly sure yet but was leaning toward something to do with businesses, Lisa immediately began thinking of ways to show me as much about the business as possible. She was excited to teach me. That is something I would have never gotten to experience if I had worked at a larger business.

Lisa empowered me during my time working at the shop both in high school and during college. I was then able to relate my first-hand marketing and business management experience to the best business practices I was studying while pursuing my undergraduate degree. Lisa valued my opinion and welcomed my suggestions and ideas. We were always trying new promotions, recipes and ways to get involved in the community. As a small business that was just starting, many things were a learning process for the whole team. Lisa not only helped me get involved with Lisa's Legit Burritos but presented me with opportunities to become in-

volved with Gardiner Main Street and events downtown."

- Courtney, LLB Manager

Change Your
Hire/Fire Mindset

"If you truly want to change your life you must first change your mind."

- Donald Altman

Transparency in Hiring

It's stressful when someone quits, or an employee termination is unavoidable. There's a scramble to cover shifts and recalibrate the staff. The process of hiring and training a replacement is nerve-wracking, even with the best processes in place.

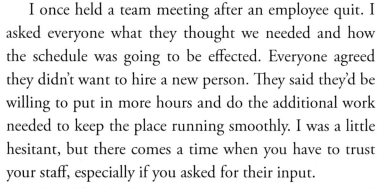

► Trust your staff.

I once held a team meeting after an employee quit. I asked everyone what they thought we needed and how the schedule was going to be effected. Everyone agreed they didn't want to hire a new person. They said they'd be willing to put in more hours and do the additional work needed to keep the place running smoothly. I was a little hesitant, but there comes a time when you have to trust your staff, especially if you asked for their input.

My staff picked up the slack, and the place ran well for months. Eventually, fatigue started setting in. I asked again if we should hire, and this time the answer was yes. We agreed I'd do the initial interviews and then I'd have candidates return to the restaurant for a working interview during the lunch rush. I'd be there to say "hi," but I wouldn't stick around.

I wanted the staff to have an opportunity to get to know candidates and get a feel for how they worked. This was important, as they'd be the ones interacting on a daily basis.

My employees had terrific insight. They'd report back with comments such as, "It was quiet, and she just stood there" and "she didn't ask what she could be doing - I don't think she's a good fit." There were other times when they'd say, "Wow! She's so great! She jumped right in and helped out even when she didn't know what to do. I think you should hire her, and she's worth more than minimum wage."

I made sure to let candidates know the working interview was a two-way street. Some found after a lunch shift they didn't want a job in food service - it just wasn't a good fit. When this happened, I'd buy them lunch and thank them for their honesty.

Glean as much information as possible before you hire.

Try to make the hiring process as positive an experience as possible. Remind yourself it's an opportunity to find qualities in a new person that perhaps the former person was lacking. It is the perfect time to reevaluate the schedule and skill sets of your staff and discuss with your group what you need for continued success.

> When you're wrong,
> admit it, fix it and move on.

I got a message from a customer that their dinner order had been royally screwed up. They were super frustrated and were venting to me in an email. I immediately apologized, thanked them for reaching out and gave them a gift certificate on the house. To improve and avoid similar issues in the future, I discussed the situation with the staff.

Sometimes, I'd learn a customer's story wasn't entirely true. Other times, I'd learn of a staffing problem or shortage that needed addressing. I gave my employees the authority to fix issues as they came up. For example, if we messed up an order, the policy was to remake the item immediately and not charge the customer. In some situations, we'd include a gift certificate on top of the fixed order.

I often communicated the vision of the company and our number one goal: customer happiness. Employees understood that every time they gave something away for free, they had to work twice as hard because the order wasn't contributing to their salary. They never once abused the ability to give away food. In fact, they were occasionally more conservative than I was.

Transparency in Firing

A friend of mine acquired staff through the purchase of a business. She quickly learned one of her inherited employees was toxic. The new owner documented the issues, gave a formal, written warning, and offered the employee a chance to correct her behavior and save her job. It was eventually clear that the relationship could not continue. My friend sat the employee down, explained the issues one last time, and officially fired her. She described to me a nerve-racking process. "You know what you have to do. You follow the proper procedures, so you know you've protected yourself legally, but there's an emotional piece to this process that doesn't have a checklist."

> Feelings can't be separated from the process, but they can be managed.

In the end, my friend had to follow her gut even though it hurt her heart. "While I was going through a process that spanned weeks, I was constantly thinking about the side effects of keeping her or letting her go, both in the short and long term. I wondered, what will the town think? What will my clients think? Will this decision hurt my business?" I had to talk out every potential action with myself. Just giving a warning, which is the first step on the path to termination, can lead to bad feelings."

I found myself asking questions like, "How is it going to affect her when she's no longer employed here?" I knew it would hurt her. I saw her as an employee and a person. I'd met her family. My heart tugged at me to look past her poor performance, but I knew my business needed to work. I had to consider my other employees and the organization as a whole. Keeping her on staff might have led to others quitting.

> Consider the health of
> your business ecosystem.

As soon as one question is answered, several more may come up. It can take awhile to reach the point of termination. You may try switching people around, fixing the environment or mediating between employees and customers. When there is an issue with an employee, it can feel like trying to solve a puzzle with a piece that just doesn't fit.

> Create a procedure and follow it.

Ultimately, your employees are looking to you to fix whatever is wrong. The consequences of your actions (or inaction) will have lasting effects. Circumstances need to be carefully considered. Always talk to your lawyer. Document the shit out of things. Sign things with a witness. Letting someone go needs to be done objectively. Your feelings might keep you up at night, but if you follow your gut and the proper procedures, you will know you were just in the process.

Transparency Networking

"The most important single ingredient in the formula of success is knowing how to get along with people."

-Theodore Roosevelt,
26th President of the United States

Everyone has a story, passions, and expertise. It might not appear obvious by the way they dress or the job title they hold. That's what makes networking so much fun! If you resist stereotyping people and truly see each person as someone who possesses something unique and wonderful, many doors will open for you.

Don't get me wrong - there are total assholes out there. Still, I try to treat everyone with respect. I look beyond the moment with the understanding that the experience might serve a valuable function in the future. I put everyone in my mental Rolodex of contacts. Chances are high I'll be talking to someone - weeks or months later - and make a connection.

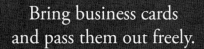

> Bring business cards
> and pass them out freely.

Attending a networking event when you don't know anyone can feel overwhelming. Even I, the most extroverted of beings, get a little stressed when I walk into an event. I go prepared with a pocket full of business cards to hand out to everyone I meet. I remind myself that everyone is feeling the same way - we all came here to meet new people. I scan the room and try to find someone I've met before.

Find the food.

If I don't recognize anyone, I find the food. Chatting about the food selection is always an easy way to begin a conversation. Add "By the way, my name is Lisa," and it's easy to go on from there.

Smile and make eye contact.

You'll put your nervous self at ease, and you'll also come across as warm and inviting to others. Remember to smile before you enter a room and when you begin a new conversation.

Don't be afraid to join in.

There is nothing wrong with participating in a conversation and waiting for a natural break in the chatter to introduce yourself. In most cases, the people who are already speaking will enjoy the interruption because it gives them a chance to meet someone new.

▶ Comment on someone's attire.

I often wear a pair of Dansko shoes with a paint-spattered pattern. They're an instant conversation starter. People say, "Wow! Where did you get those shoes?" Everyone loves to hear they have great fashion sense, and it's guaranteed to put a smile on their face.

▶ Ask what they do, where they work or how they heard about the event.

Don't make it your mission to talk to everyone in the place. Try to make 2-3 good connections or set a goal for the number of business cards you'd like to collect. Bribe yourself with a sweet treat if you hit your target.

If a list of attendees is published before the event, review it and identify who you need to meet. Make it your mission to connect with them.

▶ Set a time limit for yourself.

If the networking event is 2 hours, I promise myself

I'll stay for the first hour. If I made an effort to get there, I need to make the most of the time.

I use every opportunity to practice my networking skills and hone my ability to connect with strangers. Whenever I check out of a store, I ask the clerk how s/he is doing and listen to the response. I ask a few follow-up questions to keep the conversation going as I'm completing the transaction. It's less intimidating to practice these skills in everyday interactions. People love to hear themselves talk, and you can learn a lot by asking open-ended questions.

As an early arriver, you have a chance to engage one-on-one with a few attendees before all of the noise and bustle sets in. You also have the luxury of making the first impression in people's minds before they are drowning in business cards and handshakes. In fact, you might have so many productive conversations in the first hour that you don't have to stick around for the full networking event.

If you get someone's business card, take a few minutes in the following days to send them a quick note. Make sure to reference something you talked about during your exchange. A generic, "nice to meet you" email won't make you memorable.

The goal of the email is to establish a longer lasting connection. As you build your network, you will want to be known as a person who follows up. You know those people who say they'll send you something and then you never hear from them again? You don't trust them - don't be that person!

► Make good on your promises.

Even if it's as simple as "I just wanted to follow up and let you know that I'm still working on it. I'll be in touch once I have more info for you."

► Keep the lines of communication open.

People appreciate the effort because it is rare these days. If you had a great conversation, ask the person if they want to meet for coffee. Relationships take time to cultivate and in person is always better! Ask your conversation partner the best way to stay in touch. Some people like email or phone, while others prefer social networks like LinkedIn or even Facebook.

Develop a reputation as a resource.

When you're known as a strong resource, people remember to turn to you for suggestions, ideas, and recommendations for professional services. This keeps you visible.

Have a clear understanding of what you do, why you do it, and for whom.

What makes you or your business special or different from others doing the same thing? To get referrals, you must first have a clear understanding of what you do. Only then can you effectively communicate your business to others.

> ## Know how others can help.

Be able to articulate what you're looking for or what kind of aid you need. Too often, people in conversations are asked, "How can I help you?" and no immediate answer comes to mind. That's a missed opportunity.

> ## If large crowds are intimidating, choose more intimate events or visit with your downtown neighbors.

At least quarterly, I'd take a few hours and go into each business in downtown Gardiner. This was one of my ways of networking within the business community. I'd stop by and say hi. We'd talk about how business was going and brainstorm ideas for making it better. I went out of my way to approach fellow business owners because they didn't necessarily have the means to be able to get out from behind their counters to network. Plus, I just loved talking to people!

> ## Keep your eye on the long game.

These visits energized me and made me even more excited to be part of a historic downtown. Over time, they deepened my connection to the community.

> **Professional relationships take time to develop. Nurture them.** ◀

The first Christmas Ian was gone was very stressful financially. My staff worked so hard and I wanted to give them all a million dollars but I knew we were going into the dead of winter and I needed to be very conservative with my spending. I didn't have the safety net of my husband's income any longer.

I reached out to a consignment shop owner and said, "I didn't know if you would be interested in doing some bartering? I'm trying to find a creative way to give my employees Christmas gifts this year. I'd give you, say, $50 in gift certificates to the burrito shop to use for yourself or give as gifts and you would give me $50 in gift certificates to your store to give as presents to my employees." If I hadn't taken the time to cultivate the relationship over the years, there is no way I would have felt comfortable asking for such a thing!

> **Get involved in your community.** ◀

Find a nonprofit whose mission you're passionate about and get involved! You don't have to give away money or product - your time is also valuable. You'll help strengthen your community and build leadership skills, all while growing your network.

▶ **Volunteering opens doors.**

I served on the board of the organization that led the revitalization effort of downtown Gardiner. A vice-president of a local bank and a manager at a local staffing agency also served on this board. Through my volunteer efforts, I gained access to valuable knowledge just by sitting around the table with them.

▶ **Be creative with underutilized space.**

While volunteering, I learned from the Director of our local library that they dreamt of having a little community bookstore in town. But in addition to the financial challenges they'd face, they didn't know how they'd staff it. So when I bought my 1800's building, complete with beautiful, built in bookshelves tucked just off the dining room, I invited the library to join us.

It was as simple as adding a button on our cash register. Each month, I totaled the book sales and wrote them a check. A library volunteer came in weekly to restock the shelves, price items and organize. The only overhead was a small monthly rent.

People waiting for food would peruse the books and often found a new read. Other customers coming in for a book would smell our delicious food cooking and order something. It was a win-win!

Networking doesn't have to happen at an organized event while wearing a suit. It can take place anywhere, with anyone.

"*Lisa taught me how networking helps people grow. It started when she took me to the Chamber of Commerce's Business After Hours event. I'd expressed to Lisa I wanted to find another job. At the event, I collected people's cards and followed up. After I took a new position, I'd no longer just show up at events; I'd bring company materials with me. I began making the most of the events. It just grew from there. She sees everything as limitless. It is so inspiring. I no longer wanted to settle for my job as a receptionist - the sky was now the limit. Since meeting Lisa, I've increased my pay by almost $10/hour.*"

- Ashley Stradtman

Unintentional Networking can Generate Big Rewards

"Formal education will make you a living;
self-education will make you a fortune."
                                    - Jim Rohn

Long before I started LLB, I was fed up sitting in an office. I called my friend Eliza and told her I needed to be self-employed. I couldn't stand coming into an office and being trapped there 8 hours a day. I wanted the freedom to kick ass at work, do some laundry and then go back to dominating at work. She was working in the coffee and tea import business and encouraged me to go out on my own. With her guidance and a lot of self-education, I launched an online company, baxtertea.com.

I operated the business out of my home office in Gardiner. I loved being my own boss, but it was socially isolating. Being a very outgoing person, I struggled being home all of the time. I decided to join the promotions committee of Gardiner Main Street. I loved volunteering for various events throughout the year, including the tree lighting at Christmas and trick-or-treating on Halloween.

The Gardiner Main Street organization was created to foster the downtown's "economic and cultural vitality through concentrated efforts of design, organization, promotion and economic revitalization while protecting the city's unique historic character."
- gardinermainstreet.org

Kara was new to Gardiner and had recently purchased a beautiful, historic building in the heart of downtown. She was looking to open a high-end consignment bridal boutique and bakery/tea shop. Kara envisioned brides coming in with their families and having tea parties while they tried on dresses. When she bounced her idea off of a few local folks, they all insisted she and I connect.

Although I was confused as to how wedding dresses and tea parties in the same space would go, I agreed to explore the idea further. After all, she wasn't going to charge me very much rent, and it would give my online business a face locally.

Kara's professional background was in planning, but she made the most heavenly cupcakes. She saw a hole in the Gardiner market, so we teamed up to breathe life into an empty storefront.

While I initially hadn't set out to operate a business with a retail location, I was committed to developing strong connections within my community. Because I wasn't just sitting at home by myself filling orders, I met Kara and the rest is history.

You never know where unintentional networking will lead you.

On a warm summer morning, I went yard saling in Hallowell for tea cups to use in the new space. When I happened upon a sale, and it's hostess, Deb, I enthusiastically shared with her my plans to expand my online business into a beautiful, historic storefront location, complete with original hardwood floors, a tin ceiling, and crystal chandeliers. I was feeling very excited!

Deb told me she was a music teacher at a local high school and wanted to know if I'd thought about doing fundraising with my products. She said she was tired of having her kids sell the same old wrapping paper and overpriced candy bars. Deb thought a locally owned coffee and tea company would be an awesome addition to their usual fundraising lineup. She was quick to point out how it might also help me build a local customer base for my new retail location.

She had incredible passion in her voice when she talked about being a music teacher. She explained how important a successful fundraiser was to her program. Her enthusiasm was infectious, and it got me excited! She promised if I added a fundraising program to my company, she'd be the first person on the schedule the coming fall. The more she spoke about the possibility, the more I believed in my ability to make the idea a reality.

Before Deb was done telling me about her challenges with fundraising, I was brainstorming what products I wanted to include (I had over 75 in inventory) and what kind of margins I could live with for this venture. After a frenzy of back-and-forth questioning to further understand what elements were required for success, I left completely energized.

 A simple conversation catapulted my business into an unexpected, exciting direction.

I rationalized my decision to go ahead with the fund-raising idea by acknowledging I was on a roll. I'd already successfully created an online business and was ready to branch out with a retail location. Of course I could add another division to the company!

What's the worst thing that could happen? Losing money on marketing materials I developed?! Many people might argue with me about lost time, but I don't believe in that train of thought at all.

 Every experience is an opportunity to learn and grow.

My dad calls any failure or setback "the tuition you pay in life." Risks are not only about doing great things professionally. They also stretch you personally. Every process is a skill building opportunity.

I could have purchased the tea set, said thank you, and gone on the next yard sale, but because I am always looking to increase my network and reach my next level of greatness, I instead talked about my plans for expanding my online business into a retail location.

> **The devil is always in the details.**

As soon as I got home, I placed the beautiful tea set on my dining room table, grabbed a notebook and got to work. I wrote down all my best selling products and pulled out my Excel spreadsheet to check margins and play with the numbers.

Deb told me I'd need to give 40% of sales to the school. Knowing I'd have high volumes coming in and that I'd have 4-6 weeks to process orders, I decided I could live with tighter margins. I could wait until all the orders were in before purchasing product. This meant I wouldn't have to tie up all my cash in product before I was able to sell it.

To ensure my branding was consistent, I engaged a professional designer to create my fundraising materials and had them printed at a local shop.

As promised, Deb was the first teacher to sign up to do a fundraiser. She had over 100 kids participating and invited me into her music classes to introduce myself and the product. She wanted me to get the kids as fired up about coffee and tea as I was the day I said YES to creating the program!

The fundraisers were a big success. The number of schools and organizations involved grew organically. I'd get calls from people saying, "I bought some coffee from Sally in Brewer, and I love it! I think this would be a great fundraiser to do at my church. Can you send me some information?" My answer? "Of course! I'd love to send you some information!" Baxter Tea helped 50+ schools and nonprofits across Maine raise money for much-needed trips and activities each year.

The Importance of Feedback

"Most receive advice, only the wise profit from it."

- Publilius Syrus

It's so important to get feedback from a broad spectrum of people. You want to hear from potential customers, mentors, other business owners and your family and friends. But at some point, you need to *stop* soliciting advice.

I see so many entrepreneurs get stuck in the acquisition of knowledge phase when considering an idea. They ask for feedback from every source, even misguided ones.

> Process what's been said, then make a decision. The purpose of collecting input is to inform ACTION!

Be mindful of whom you're asking for advice, feedback, and guidance. For example, if you're looking to add a peanut butter cheesecake burrito to your menu, don't ask people with a peanut allergy if the idea appeals to them.

Don't just ask people, "Do you like this idea?" You'll encourage a broad, non-focused answer. To solicit the most helpful feedback, ask specific questions.

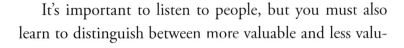

> Learn how to sort the feedback you receive.

It's important to listen to people, but you must also learn to distinguish between more valuable and less valuable information. Pay attention to the demographics of the person you're asking as they relate to the information you're gathering. Say you're looking to open a gaming lounge. Your customer discovery should give more consideration to feedback offered by a 12-year-old, avid, gamer who spends every penny he earns on his hobby than to opinions expressed by me, a serial entrepreneur and single mother. While I have a lot of valuable knowledge to convey, he is your target audience.

If you're dealing with a serious business problem and are seeking feedback, find a trusted mentor to help guide you.

> Ask for input, but assign value based on its source. ◀

"Lisa thinks about business 24/7. At the same time, she's a mom, and she's doing mom things, but business is always on her mind. Most people thrive on getting approval for their business concept and achieving early success in the business. Not Lisa. She thrives by people saying "you're going to fail," and then she sets out to prove them wrong.

Once we were in the veterinarian's office with her dog, Shelby. Lisa was telling the Dr. about her newest venture, a Mexican restaurant in Gardiner. He ever-so-slightly rolled his eyes. He asked how she could do it. He had come to the conclusion that since she wasn't Mexican, she'd never run a restaurant or worked in the industry, there was no way she could be success-ful. She didn't let his comments phase her. If anything, they fueled her to work even harder. She was eager to add him to the list of people she'd call up one day to let them know she'd made it, despite their uninspiring comments."

- Maria Liberatore

Fiscal Responsibility

"Successful people understand that to get results most people don't get, they have to be willing to do what most people aren't willing to do."

- Patrik Edblad

I was very fortunate to grow up in a household with financially savvy parents. They understood how to make money work for them - as opposed to them working for it. My parents had a successful family business and were able to send their children to private school, kindergarten through high school.

My mom is very diligent with her receipts and keeps meticulous records. My siblings and I undoubtedly learned some financial habits through osmosis. She maintained separate accounts for everything. Mom displayed the same level of financial prowess at home as she did keeping the books at Dad's office.

When we wanted something, we were told by our parents to save. But my parents didn't stop there - they took the extra step and showed us how.

▶ Set financial goals.

As a family, we would put our spare change into big jars. At the end of the summer, we'd roll it up, cash it in, and use the money to go to Santa's Village, an amusement park in New Hampshire. This was our big family trip of the year. Looking back, it's clear we never had enough change to finance those trips completely, but as kids, the process taught us about having goals and saving for them.

I remember getting home from babysitting one night and going into my parent's room to tell them how much money I'd made. I was so excited! Immediately, Dad said, "Give me 10%." I was like, "wait, what?!" He explained to me that night that I should save 10% of every dollar I earned. This practice lays the groundwork for financial security. Create a budget that includes saving and stick to it.

Plan for the future now. ◀

If you save, you will be prepared for unexpected events, such as when your car breaks down. Saving increases your level of financial preparedness. Having money set aside to cover emergencies will go a long way to help you avoid unnecessary debt and financial stress. I keep 3-6 months worth of expenses in reserve, and I've been very grateful for this practice during challenging financial times. Also, you never know when an opportunity will present itself. Savings will help you worry less about the financial road-blocks to an idea so you can focus more on the details.

As kids, this motto applied to most things we wanted. We were taught to respect financial freedom and understood that it comes at a cost. Often, the cost was delayed gratification. After saving and saving, it was hard watching my account balance plunge to almost empty following a big purchase. This made me question how badly I wanted some things and also created a sense of hustle in me. I always search for the best deal, and once I've spent down an account, I'm eager to get it growing again.

When Ian and I were married, we had a goal of buying acreage and eventually building a camp in Northern Maine. We'd started saving money when we found 10 acres in Lee for 10k. It was such an amazing deal, we knew we needed to jump on it. But we didn't have the money saved yet, and no bank wanted to finance such a small dollar amount. We had to get creative.

Because we were both very disciplined with money, I knew if we just had a year, we could save the money we needed. When a Bank of America credit card offer appeared in the mailbox promising zero interest for 13 months and a 4% transaction fee, I couldn't believe it! We could get an interest free loan for only $400. We just needed to reorganize our budget to ensure we could pay the $867 a month needed to avoid any interest kicking in and get the best deal possible.

We committed to a new budget and went for it! I've seen people who earn a lot more than I do struggle with finances. I've also watched otherwise successful businesses fail because the owners lacked financial knowledge and fiscal restraint. It takes time, diligence and commitment to develop these fundamental skills.

Audrey's Story

I was in my senior year of college when I went looking on Craigslist for gift ideas for my mom's birthday. I found a beautiful tourmaline ring for sale and reached out to the seller. I received an immediate response from Audrey, who asked if I'd be willing to come to her house as she was home caring for her baby and couldn't leave.

I was excited to be purchasing such a lovely piece of jewelry for pennies on the dollar, so I happily agreed and made the 20-minute drive out of town. Audrey's relief that I was there to buy her ring was palpable. She invited me in and introduced me to her beautiful baby girl, Alyssa, who was crawling around on the floor. I learned Audrey and I were the same age and she'd also been a student at UMaine. When she got pregnant with Alyssa, she got married and dropped out of school.

The ring she was selling was her engagement ring. Her husband had left and she was desperate to buy diapers and food. They were in credit card debt and her car was unreliable. As she told me her story, it was clear she was stressed, but she wasn't looking for pity. Her incredible strength was obvious. She was determined to take care of herself and her child, and she was doing what she needed to do.

I left there with the ring, plus a bunch of other, random items I didn't need, because there was no way I wasn't giving her all the cash I had on me. Here I was, living in a beautiful, four bedroom house by myself, going to college and having fun every weekend. My biggest stressor was deciding which bar to visit. I wasn't worried about whether or not I had money to feed my child or put gas in my car. Our worlds couldn't have been more different, and I felt very grateful for the resources available to me.

Audrey and I became friends following our chance encounter. In time, she landed a great job at Husson College and clawed her way out of the debt leftover from her marriage. I'd met her at a financial low point but her fierce determination and independence served her well going forward. She returned every favor and then some, and she taught me it doesn't matter where you are in life - if you want to, you can become financially stable!

Self Care

"Rest & self-care are so important. When you take time to replenish your spirit, it allows you to serve others from the overflow. You cannot serve from an empty vessel."

- Eleanor Brown

There were days when nothing seemed to go right. No matter how hard I tried, things just wouldn't come together. When this happened, I'd take it as a sign that I needed to hit the reset button. I'd treat myself to a latte or get the pedicure I'd wanted for months but for which I hadn't allowed myself the time.

Taking a break means creating an opportunity for self-care. I'm here to say it again - self-care is a thing everyone needs and deserves. This includes you! It doesn't have to be an expensive or time-consuming event. Sometimes it's as simple as giving yourself permission to feel defeated by the task at hand and finding something else to conquer, like a decadent cherry cheese danish from Bagel Central.

I have been described as a workaholic, and although it might appear that way when you see me in meetings during the day and then get an email from me at 2 am, I do make sure to find balance. If I can't sleep in the middle of the night, I'd rather feel productive and know when I wake up in the morning, I'm already ahead on emails.

"Work and play are the same. When you're following your energy and doing what you want all the time, the distinction between work and play dissolves."
- Shakti Gawain

I don't schedule my life around working 8-5 with rest of the day as family time. Instead, I blend all the hours of the day together. For example, I don't schedule meetings before 8:30 am. This way, if Dorian sleeps in or we're just not moving quickly, I don't have to rush our morning routine. If I complete the professional tasks that need my attention, I shift to something else, such as grocery shopping or a trip to Target.

> ## You *must* make time for self-care and insist your friends do the same!

I once called my friend, Jesse, totally overwhelmed. It was the "I'm at the end of my rope" calls when we're not even sure why we're calling, only that we need to be heard.

It wasn't even 9 am and I was losing at life. I was having a difficult time turning it around. My general positivity just wasn't cutting it.

> ## When all else fails, take a mommy time-out!

Jesse gave me permission to do something I knew I needed to do but hadn't. She reminded me: "You need to take care of yourself, Lisa! Screw everything else. If you fall apart, there is nothing left - you're keeping it all together.

Can you please do me a favor and go to Starbucks right now? Get your favorite drink, sit down and focus on enjoying it."

I took her advice. Those 10 minutes of calm and reflection allowed me to regroup and move forward with the rest of my day.

▶ Daytime drinking is sometimes the cure!

When I was completely overwhelmed by the changing dynamics in my marriage, the stress of running two restaurants and the demands of being a mom, I'd call my friend Sarah and schedule a playdate. I'd sit, enjoy a glass of wine (or three!) and relax with her while our kids played.

Life has changed a lot since then, but playdates still give me the energy to head back into battle. They are often the perfect antidote to whatever is ailing me.

▶ Self-care is not a luxury. It's a necessity.

Practicing self-care allows me to step back and really focus on my son's happiness and our well-being. It means living with intention and not just going through the motions, straining to keep my head above water. It includes planning and having fun adventures and making sure we spend as much time as possible laughing and hugging.

We went through a period of time when Dorian wanted "happy cake" every day. I found a recipe for a 'cake in a mug' and we'd make them together. He and I would sing Happy Birthday, clap and blow out the candle. Seeing him smile gave me such strength!

Make sure to schedule downtime.

For me, downtime comes in the form of shopping. I love to find a deal, so I keep a running list of things I need and allocate time to browse the aisles. It's one of my favorite forms of relaxation.

There are many ways to find your footing when you feel overwhelmed.

I do yoga and listen to music. Miley Cyrus' "The Climb" was my go-to song for a long time. The lyrics resonated with me. I like to crank up the volume and get to work cleaning. Cleaning is satisfying because the results are immediate - unlike growing a business or raising a child!

When my confidence wanes, I cope by addressing clutter in my physical environment. I pack up outgrown toys and clothes and pass them on to someone in need. It helps heal me when I give things away in the spirit of making someone else's life better, and having a tidier environment always improves my mental outlook.

William Morris said it best: *"Have nothing in your house that you do not know to be useful, or believe to be beautiful."*

> ## Accept that multitasking is sometimes necessary.

Being a mom and a business owner is mentally taxing. Most working women remain responsible for the majority of the household tasks. Many do the grocery shopping, make appointments, help with homework, cook, clean and do the laundry. The list goes on and on.

It's very easy to slip into the habit of constantly multi-tasking. For example, I sometimes find myself half-listening to my kid while putting the groceries away. Then I remember I left a load of laundry in the washer. Now I'm worried the clothes might smell like mold and I'll have to wash them again... And, oh my gosh, what about the three other loads I should have done?!

Before I know it, I've completely lost track of the present moment, and I have no idea what my child has just said to me. But multitasking has a place. When I get in the zone, I get things done, and a sense of control is returned to my life. I try to balance these times by regularly shifting my attention.

Practice mindfulness.

Mindfulness is not something that comes naturally or easily to me. I have to work at it. When I'm able, I remember to take a deep breath and focus, for example, on putting a puzzle together if that's what Dorian wants to do. When I sit down, I feel the floor beneath me. I take in his big brown eyes and his huge smile. I notice how soft his skin is next to mine and how wonderful it feels to be with him. When I reach over and tickle him, I wrap him in a big hug and savor the feelings that rush over me.

Turn inward. Discover what makes you feel empowered and then DO IT.

I don't think people spend enough time saying positive and uplifting things to themselves or others. I'm amazed by how many people focus on what is flawed or needs to be fixed. Give yourself as much praise and love as possible before giving to others.

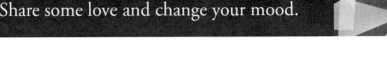

Share some love and change your mood.

One morning, I stopped by the restaurant to do the draw and found it was off. I spent a lot of time trying to figure out where the error occurred. Counting pennies for the 20th time, while simultaneously trying to keep Dorian quasi-occupied, was just too much. By the time I left, I was completely annoyed and in a terrible mood. I knew I didn't want to continue feeling that way, so I made a conscious decision to focus my energy on something positive.

Dorian and I delivered flowers and cookies to friends who were struggling with bad days of their own. It was great having his help spreading cheer, and I felt I was teaching a valuable lesson: when you can't find your smile, put one on someone else's face. Self care is not always about focusing on self; sometimes it comes in the form of serving others.

Be passionate about what you do.

When you're passionate about the work you do, it radiates to everyone and everything around you. People told me how I lit up when talking about LLB. My eyes would get bright and it was clear how much I believed in and cared about my business.

When a passion fades, you owe it to yourself to reignite it or pass the torch.

I loved LLB- it was my life. I was and will always be so proud of the restaurant I built and the people who worked for me. But there came a time when what I needed was a new challenge. I went on a search for what would fire me up again. Creating a licensing agreement became my new focus. It was the thing I couldn't stop thinking about, the idea I'd gladly lose sleep over.

Don't force something that isn't coming naturally.

When an idea or situation ceases to yield satisfaction or success, recognize it for what it is and find a way to move on. When you connect with your passion, every-thing flows in your life. It's not always sunshine and ros-es, but things start to come together and synergy appears. When I began pursuing a licensing agreement, a new way forward came into view. My passion took me in an ex-citing direction and allowed me to pass LLB's operations torch to someone who cared and who could attend to the appropriate details.

Don't be afraid to fail - or succeed.

Voice your ideas. Talk about your passions with others. The world can't help make your dreams come true if nobody knows what they are!

Details Matter

"It's not about the card you're dealt, but how you play the hand."

> *- Randy Pausch,*
> *The Last Lecture*

On occasion, I'd drive down to Gardiner to check on LLB and make everything was running smoothly. My name was on the sign, and even though I'd stepped away from day-to-day operations, it was still my reputation on the line. As owner, I took full responsibility for the good, the bad and the ugly, even when I wasn't directly involved.

During one such visit, I went into the bathroom and was appalled by how dirty it was. It clearly hadn't been cleaned in days. Two staff members and I crammed into the single restroom. While they watched, I got down on my hands and knees and scrubbed the toilet. I reminded them of my standards in the restaurant and showed them the level of cleanliness I expected.

> By example, leaders must demonstrate the strength of their work ethic and the degree of detail they expect from others.

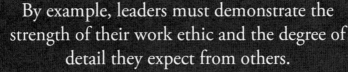

For me, this wasn't about rank. I reminded my staff that my job as owner was to focus on the big picture and creating a licensing agreement. I was working hard to bring in customers. I needed them to focus on doing their jobs - including cleaning - so all of us could count on a paycheck.

Every time I stopped in after that, the bathroom was in perfect order. Word got around to the staff that details mattered to me. I helped them understand that customers pay attention to everything, and we had to also.

> Customers are the lifeblood of your business.
> Give them every reason to sing your praises.

Occasionally when calling an employee out on something left undone, I'd hear the excuse, "I didn't have time." That doesn't cut it with me. I pay my employees by the hour, and "closing time" isn't a fixed amount of time - it's a range.

Leading by example, I handled the issue by doing the job myself - and timing it - as the employee watched. My staff was always surprised by how quickly tasks got completed.

To achieve the life you dream of, you need to care. You need to care about the little details - the ones that don't seem important in the grand scheme but are the very things upon which you will build your success.

"With Lisa, you get the best of both worlds. She is artistically minded, but she processes information in an orderly, chronological way. She can envision the big picture, but she doesn't lose track of the details. These skills can be learned by listening to her and watching her work."

- Jamie Tremblay,
Blush Bridal and Formal

Free to Find Me

"Careers are a jungle gym, not a ladder."
- Sheryl Sanberg

The jungle gym model perfectly describes the way my professional career has evolved.

I have a Bachelor's degree in Child Development and I went on to get a Master's in College Administration with a concentration in Educational Leadership. For a time, I worked in Career Services as a Recruitment Specialist. I helped students choose a career path and taught them how to 'dress for success.'

> Think outside the box.

I was unhappy in my traditional, 9-5 career. I wanted more flexibility and autonomy than a job working for someone else could provide. I left my office position and began my entrepreneurial adventures by starting a tea/coffee business. I also started investing in real estate, became a notary and received training as birthing doula! I was willing to take a leap of faith. I left an unsatisfying job and went on to experience many beautiful things.

Eventually, I created two restaurants and have since opened a coworking space. The varied skills I acquired with each undertaking have helped shape who I am today. Each profession I tried required some level of self-education and networking.

Growing up, I wasn't naturally adept in math and science. I battled dyslexia and struggled with reading comprehension. Unlike my siblings, all of whom have doctorates, I wasn't destined for the medical field. My training/ education has a much broader application. My goal in life is to find happiness. I understood that a job requiring me to show up on a schedule and ask for permission for time off was not for me. I knew that I was - and always would be - on a quest to discover more in life. What I was looking to get out of my life - professional or otherwise - wasn't going to come from someone else.

> Greatness doesn't come without failure. ◄

I have never created boundaries for myself. I never let anything hold me back. Everything in my life - from college and business to marriage and motherhood - I try my hardest and have the confidence to go after what I want. If it doesn't work out, it's ok. I know I will have learned something and I just move on. When you realize you deserve greatness, you see everything as another step toward your goal of awesomeness.

Core Operating Principles

▶ Take care of yourself.

For me, taking care of myself means eating healthy foods, exercising regularly and getting plenty of SLEEP! I love to sleep and need it. Even as a kid, I would put myself to bed when I was tired. It's crucial for my health and wellbeing to be rested.

▶ Trust in a higher power.

When facing difficult or challenging situations, remember that the crazy roller coaster ride you're on is necessary - that's how you get to the high point where you can see for miles - you'll look back and find yourself saying, "Oh, wow! I'm so thankful my husband walked out. None of these awesome things would have happened had he stayed…"

▶ Learn to silence your brain.

Once, when upset over a crisis developing at LLB, I was carpooling home from an event with a friend. My anxiety was getting the best of me, and I was coping by talking. As we drove along, I asked a million questions, none of them necessary or related to each other. My friend finally said, "Lisa, you need to stop talking! You need to be silent for a few minutes. You've got a lot on your mind, but you need just to STOP."

I was a little pissed, but I knew he was right. I shut my mouth, took a deep breath and looked out the window. I focused on my view of the night sky and watched the bright moon follow us as we traveled the highway in silence. I concentrated on my breathing and regained a sense of calm.

▶ Learn to think independently.

Too much structure kills my creativity. Yes, there is a formula for starting a business, which includes drafting a business plan, making cash flow projections, etc. I value and respect that type of structure, but when it comes to executing, I need the method to be organic.

▶ Just show up.

Some days it is all you can do. Don't worry about looking pretty. Just arrive - and who cares if it's late. Some people rely on a buddy system for accountability. Others find success with simple rules and rewards. Find a thing or system that motivates and focuses you and go for it!

▶ Do what needs to be done.

When I see something that needs to be done, I usually jump in and do it. I don't waste time floating through life, drifting aimlessly from one task to another and wondering what I'm doing. Whether it's an order that needs to be filled or paperwork that needs to be filed, when I have work to do, I make a list and then execute it.

Getting things done and crossing them off of a list is a great confidence booster. List making is a powerful tool for measuring the progress you're making in your life. At the end of the day, when I lay my head down, I know what I've done with my time, and that's a deeply satisfying feeling.

Action feeds on itself. Each small victory propels you toward bigger goals. There's a snowball effect: you just get going and all of a sudden, you've accomplished so much!

I once read an article about how people dread unloading the dishwasher. We spend more time procrastinating than it takes just to do it. I timed it one day to see for myself. In my head, it seemed like an eternity. In reality, it took less than 5 minutes.

▶ Take your job seriously.

I have so many friends who start little side business as a way to supplement their family's income. All too often, I watch them fail. They don't take the time to create a business plan, nor do they learn how to manage inventory and the actual start-up costs. Instead, they just start sewing and throw up an Etsy site, doing it on a wing and a prayer. Don't invest all your time and money only to watch your business die a slow death.

▶ If you don't have a solid foundation, you can't expect your business to thrive.

I watch as they freak out because they didn't set up the right systems to execute their new business's obligations in a timely fashion. Murphy's Law is always in effect at the worst time. Babies get sick, or the internet goes down - it just adds to the chaos. My friends create unnecessary stress for themselves because they haven't thought their ideas through to completion.

▶ Create a dedicated workspace.

You need an office. You need a dedicated space - not the kitchen table - where you can go to and focus. So many people, particularly with the advent of technology, think you don't need a dedicated space in which to work. In my experience, that's just not true. I believe everyone needs a place to organize not only thoughts but paperwork.

▶ Get organized.

Make to-do lists and keep a calendar. I have friends who swear by bullet journaling. Whatever the system, find one that works for you and employ it.

▶ Develop a can do, no fear attitude.

Don't get scared away by difficult tasks. Just go for it, even if you don't know how to jump in and figure it out. There is no reward without risk. Yes, you might make less money than you'd hoped for. And it's true; things don't usually turn out just as we expect. But regardless of the outcome, you will learn always learn something valuable from the experience of pursuing your ideas.

▶ Commit to 'it" daily.

When Dorian, who is 4, got his first Fender electric guitar (complete with amp!), he was very excited to learn to play. Not knowing how to play guitar, I sat down at the piano and began playing a few pieces composed by David Lanz.

My fingers were rusty, but within minutes, I was playing complex songs with relative ease. I recalled how many years ago, I'd struggled to learn the timing and correct finger positions for these same pieces. I was know able to play them comfortably, without much focus or effort, despite having taken my last lesson 25 years ago. In that moment, I realized my parent's insistence that I commit to a daily habit had really paid off.

▶ Read!

"Read 500 pages every day. That's how knowledge works. It builds up, like compound interest. All of you can do it, but I guarantee not many of you will do it."

- Warren Buffett

If I want to keep up with Warren Buffett and Mark Cuban, who is reported to read up to 3 hours a day, I better get reading!

I have the Medium app on my phone, so when I need to take a break, I scroll through my curated feed of articles on self-improvement, entrepreneurship, productivity, life lessons, and psychology among others. Because I read blogs, I have no clue how many pages I read, but I'm confident that the real point is to keep learning - keep introducing yourself to new ideas, knowledge, and viewpoints.

My reading habit has also helped me when it comes to networking. My exposure to a broad range of ideas and concepts means I always have something interesting to talk about with others.

► Make it look easy.

People don't need to know how long you spend researching and ruminating over your work. No one will see the hours you spent discussing the minute details, but they will see the result. All of the time dedicated to the backside of the business will help it gain momentum. When you're able to look around and know your justification for every element in your business, you're in a strong position. A well thought out model will attract others, and you'll gain recognition for your attention to detail and the value you provide.

In conclusion, there are 10,080 minutes in every week. Lost time can't be recovered, so it's best to use it wisely.

Blending Work and Family

*"Stretch out your hand and receive the world's
wide gift of joy, appreciation, and beauty."*
- Corinne Roosevelt Robinson

I was fortunate to be raised in my dad's dental office. From the time I was old enough to walk, I was at the office with my parents. My dad did the technical work and my mom ran the business side of the practice.

My jobs included calling patients to remind them of upcoming appointments, taking payments, writing receipts, scheduling appointments, cleaning, chatting with parents whose kids were being seen and, of course, a lot of filing. I used to love going into the dark room and helping develop x-rays. By the time I was 8 or 9, I was developing them on my own.

As I grew, so did my abilities. I was given more responsibility and my understanding of how to run the business expanded. I learned how to juggle a phone ringing, a patient waiting to make a payment and x-rays needing to be developed. Maintaining flow in the office required my ability to multitask, work quickly without mistakes, and communicate clearly with others.

My dad took us kids to Rotary meetings, and when he went to dental conferences, we were in tow. We were raised in the public eye, and as a result, we knew how to conduct ourselves professionally at a young age. I now understand what a huge leg up in life it was to develop these soft skills at such a young age.

When I worked as a career specialist at the University of New England, I taught students how to dress professionally, how to speak in an interview and how to manage multiple priorities at once. I helped them be adults in the professional world. For me, so much of what I taught seemed obvious. I wondered why some students had such difficulty grasping the material. But then, I'd remember that my dad raised us kids to be little professionals, so it came second nature to us.

We were still kids. We went to art camps, took piano lessons and played sports, but instead of sitting home playing Mario Cart, we were together as a family at the office. If it were quiet, we'd pull out our homework and get it done between patients. My parents showed us how to blend work and life successfully, and now I'm doing the same with Dorian.

Every year, my dad and his best friend would get together and hike Mt. Katahdin with the kids. I was responsible for developing the menu, grocery shopping and packing the food for the trip. Dad would oversee my work and give me a ride to the grocery store, but it was my job to get down in the weeds with details. I'd determine what cooking utensils we would need, which spices to bring, etc. I'd then portion and pack everything into our backpacks. Every year, we came down the mountain with way too much extra food. I considered this a good thing. Being Italian, the worse thing that could happen to you is not having enough food. Ending a meal with no leftovers is a sin!

Support

"See every difficulty as a challenge, a stepping stone, and never be defeated by anything or anyone."

- Eileen Caddy

I am fortunate to have four separate and distinct sources of support: the business community, a network of social connections, my close personal friends, and my family. This broad base helps me achieve success in all areas of my life.

The level of connection I have with someone determines which version of my story I'm willing to share. I don't want to be caught off guard or left feeling exposed. It's difficult enough navigating stressful situations in your personal or business life, let alone being confronted by an inquiry and not knowing what to say to whom. I make it a priority to consider in advance the degree of information I'm prepared to disclose.

My business community is great resource for bouncing ideas off of others or discussing economic development and civic related matters. I always feel reenergized after a meeting with them, and I often learn something new or expand my skill set.

I am lucky to have a diverse network of social connections. The depth of relationship I have with my acquaintances is a little different than what I have with friends - it's more superficial. We rely on each other when someone needs something, but we're not often in touch.

My closest personal friends are the people I reach out to when things are the worst - and when they're the best!

Finally, I am blessed to have an amazingly tightly knit family. They have my back no matter the time of day. When my personal life continued to morph before my eyes, I needed the support of my family most of all.

I sometimes wished I could have my miserable marriage back so that I could keep going with everything that was already spinning around me. I didn't want to add to or create a new life - I was already exhausted from opening two restaurants, having a baby and managing several investment properties. I was hoping Ian, Dorian and I could rest a while and maybe I could catch my breath. But - insert reality - that's not what happened.

> **Seek out support but recognize the filter you are using to process information.**

After Ian had left, I set out to line up support from the various people in my life, all of whom had very different things to offer. My family was as Pro-Lisa as you can get. At a moment's notice, they were ready to grab their pitchforks and take Ian down. It's a wonderful feeling knowing your family is on your side and that they're there for you. I continue to feel grateful for their loyalty.

Sarah, my friend, and Dorian's care provider was happily married. She offered a lot of love and a listening ear, but she couldn't relate personally to what I was going through with Ian. Still, her compassion was a calming influence during a very painful time.

> **Make the connections necessary to get what you need.**

Get the hug or grab the ear of a friend who will listen to you bitch if that's what you need to do. Find the right support person for the situation you're dealing with at the time. Good people sometimes offer poor advice, so remember to consider what lens your support person is looking through.

> **Always surround yourself with people you admire.**

It's important to have a wide range of friends with whom you can share different aspects of your life. Make sure you find the proper ratio of time to spend with each group. I need to be around my self-employed, entrepreneurial friends the most because they foster the drive in me that pushes me forward.

When I hang out with my friends who have more traditional jobs, I find myself getting complacent and thinking maybe life would be easier if I just had a position with benefits, paid time off (that's a thing?!), health insurance and help saving for retirement. Oh, how I miss those beautiful fringe benefits (and a steady paycheck).

I also remember being forced to report to someone else and feeling I wasn't in control of my destiny. It's all about trade-offs, but I do know one thing for sure: I have no regrets! I will never look back and say, "Wow, I wish I'd chased that dream." I went out and did it! I always learn something from my experiences and that's a victory in my book!

Audrey Revisited

I'd heard Audrey was back in Maine visiting family. I reflected on the first time I met her and the incredible stress she was going through. I called her up, and after many tears and barely being able to get the words out, we agreed to meet at Starbucks for a chat.

I hadn't seen her in years. She walked in radiating happiness and confidence. It gave me so much HOPE just seeing her face. She'd done it! She'd lost over 100 pounds, was in stylish clothes instead of a baggy sweatshirt, and her nails were done. She'd married the man of her dreams and had created a beautiful life for herself and Alyssa on the West Coast. She was exactly the person I needed to connect with at that moment in my life. When I'd first met her, she was barely surviving - she'd made it through, and now she was thriving!

While I was fortunate that I wasn't in the same financial position as she'd been when her marriage ended, we shared the pain of abandonment. We both experienced the fears one has for their child when looking into the dark abyss of the unknown. I no longer had sympathy for Audrey - I had genuine empathy. Seeing her and how far she'd come was the fuel I needed to pick myself up and write a new chapter in my life.

Celebrating the Next Chapter

"People are like stained-glass windows. They sparkle and shine when the sun is out, but when the darkness sets in their true beauty are revealed only if there is light from within."
- Elisabeth Kubler-Ross

When it was clear our marriage was beyond repair, Ian and I didn't fight our divorce. We chose to celebrate it. It was a new beginning for both of us. After the final hearing, I jokingly asked Ian if he wanted to grab a martini. We had toasted our wedding so I thought it was appropriate to toast getting divorced. I made him take a picture of me with my drink, and I posted it on Facebook. All of my friends knew when I posted that photo I was officially single. I also made Ian take one last selfie with me and our drinks. He rolled his eyes, but he knew it wasn't worth putting up a fight over something so small. We talked about Dorian and how amazing he is. *We were both committed to working hard so Dorian would have everything he needs in life. No matter how mad we would get at each other, we kept our son out of it.*

When the waitress asked how we wanted the check, we joked about not having had to split one in over ten years. We walked out of the restaurant together and gave each other a high-five before heading our separate ways.

I firmly believe one of the reasons I was able to handle the massively disruptive causality of divorce was because I knew I could conquer my fear of the unknown. I had done it time and time again. It began with leaving my job and starting a company. While I wasn't sure how I would do it, I knew I would survive and be better for it in the long run.

I still have my favorite wedding photos on my Facebook page. Pictures of guys I've dated since my divorce are on there, too. I don't go back and try to erase history or alter my past. You want to know who I am and why I am the way I am? Guess what? I am a product of the people I've interacted with and the relationships I've had.

Ian and I have been divorced for almost two years. You'll still see an occasional photo of us pop up on Facebook because he is still a part of my life. Whether I like it or not, he's the father of our child, and we will continue to have a relationship. We have been to hell and back for sure, but if I capture a great picture of us, I'm going to share it with the world. Your persona on Facebook needs to reflect who you are. The best part? It keeps people guessing!

Be real.

What Transparency Looks Like in Real Life

"The thing women have yet to learn is nobody gives you power. You just take it."
- Roseanne Barr

When I was younger, I didn't realize what my dad was teaching me. I now know he gave me rules for living my life.

My father liked to reduce life's guidelines to a minimum. Then he'd repeat them frequently until my siblings and I understood them. First and foremost are the big 3: who you are, where you are, and what is happening around you.

Dad's "Big Three."

Who you are - Think about who you represent. What does who you are say about your family? What might it say about your potential for the future?

Where you are - Think about what you are doing. Are you getting in trouble or getting things done?

What's happening around you - When we were younger, the question was, "Do you want to be caught by your parents where you are right now, doing what you are doing?!" This question serves as an overview. It gives you a snapshot of who you are, not who you think you are.

As I grew up, I started paying attention to the people around me. I'd ask myself, "Are these people a positive influence on me? Do they motivate or inspire me? Are they trying to better themselves and the world around them?"

If the answer was no, I knew I needed to assess how much time I was spending with them and what degree of influence I let them have.

Don't care what people think about you.

My dad is an orthodontist, and he drove a beat up piece-of-shit car, a 1983, blue Chevy Blazer. It had holes in the floorboards. It was so rusted out, but he kept that thing going. He didn't care about being judged on superficial things. He was an educated, successful man and wasn't interested in trying to impress anyone with the "things" he could buy. His distinguished medical degrees weren't on display - they were in our attic. He taught me from an early age to focus on not giving a fuck what people think. You aren't going to get everyone to love you. Just be you. Those who resonate with you will gravitate to you.

My dad is authentic. You will always know very clearly where you stand with him. He's 100% Italian, and there is no hiding what he thinks of you. I learned from him that it's better to have people underestimate you than to try to live up to someone else's image of what you should be.

My brother and sisters are brilliant. Learning came easily to them while I struggled with every grade. When I learned how to write, I wrote in perfect mirror image. I didn't do well on standardized tests, yet my siblings set records with their scores.

My parents saw this, and they worked extra hard to make sure I focused only on myself and my abilities. I didn't waste time comparing myself to others. Instead, I learned to measure my growth relative to myself, not my siblings. What would be the point? I'm not them!

I am a competitive person by nature, but instead of feeling inferior to my siblings, I was trained to compete against myself. When I was in 2nd grade, I got a B in reading, and I wrote my parents a note:

"Dear Mom and Dad, I am sorry I got a B in reading. I will not watch TV this week and will try harder. Love, Lisa."

► Focus on your strengths.

I have a natural ability to play the piano, something neither of my sibling's shares. I choose to focus on what I'm good at. Our differences are what make us unique. Be happy being you and don't waste time trying to be something or someone you aren't.

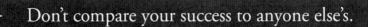

► Don't compare your success to anyone else's.

It's so easy in the age of Facebook and other media to feel like you aren't living up to the expectations of everyone on your news feed. Just STOP! Remember, the digital life is usually just smoke and mirrors. How many times have you gasped when you found out your friend is getting divorced, yet on Facebook, they looked to be the picture perfect family, one you secretly admired or wished to emulate?

Clean your lens. Don't make assumptions about people based on their appearance.

When I was growing up, my parents left town to buy new vehicles. They knew they'd have a difficult time negotiating in town because my father was a well-known doctor. Dad would dress in a tattered shirt and painter's pants. He'd bring along my mom and us three kids. We got front row seats and watched him negotiate. We were instructed to sit quietly and follow any cues, which included getting restless so he could speed up the negotiation. The sales guys always underestimated him.

So often, people focus on the wrong thing - know what you want.

My parents never revealed that they didn't need financing until they were close to sealing the deal. They had the cash, and if the sales guy wanted their money, they knew he'd find a way to make the numbers work. My parents didn't care about the sticker price. They had a number in mind and were negotiating the total price. The sticker price is important, but if you've ever look at a sales receipt, there are so many add-ons: sales tax, doc fees, and the list goes on. Dad focused on the big picture, and if he didn't get what he wanted, we walked out of the dealership.

► It takes confidence to walk away.

We'd go down the street and get McDonald's. Mom and dad knew chances were good they'd get a call (on our old-style bag car phone) after the salesman "talked to a manager," and we'd head back. Of course, there was a catch. If Dad was willing to return, they had to throw in something extra because now the deal was disrupting family time. Inevitably, we walked out of there with a new car and dealership swag. If for some reason the deal didn't work out, Dad didn't take it personally. He understood it wasn't a rejection - it was just part of the game of life.

"*The way we talk to our children becomes their inner voice.*"

- Peggy O'Mara

Epilogue

I am still growing and changing. My entrepreneurial spirit keeps pushing me to try new things.

Through a licensing agreement, awesome business partners, Ehrin and Jay, now operate LLB in Gardiner and Augusta. Dorian and I have returned to my hometown of Bangor, where I joined Scratchpad, the first seed accelerator north of Boston, Massachusetts, as Program Manager. I was the Regional Coordinator of Top Gun, the same program that helped me take LLB to new heights.

Most currently, my colleague Jason Harkins and I started a business consulting company, Fractional Executives of ME. Our focus is on assisting scalable, investment oriented companies with their customer discovery process.

In addition, Jason and I opened CoVort, Bangor's first coworking space in the heart of downtown. Surrounded by the amazing people at CoVort, I wrote this book and launched my blog and podcast with fellow CoVorter, Katrina Petersen. Life is good!